**The nurse got me seated
in the wheelchair over my protests.**
As we approached the nursery, I made
her stop. She watched as I walked stiffly
to the window looking over the bassinets.
There he was. I could spot him in a
second. I reached out to touch him, but
the glass got in my way. How long I
stood there, clawing the glass, tears
streaming down my cheeks, I do not
know.

"Good-bye," I whispered, "goodbye . . ."
The nurse, weeping herself, grabbed
me brusquely by the shoulders. "Just go,"
she shouted as she pushed me back into
the wheelchair. "Just go . . . it'll be so
much easier if you just go!" Pushing me
fiercely, she rushed out into the lobby.
The heavy swinging doors thudded shut
behind me.
MEG . . . a story you will never forget.

Meg

Meg Ashley

LIVING BOOKS
Tyndale House Publishers, Inc.
Wheaton, Illinois

Library of Congress
Catalog Card Number
79–65027
ISBN 0–8423–0175–5,
paper
Copyright © 1979 by
Meg Ashley.
All rights reserved.
First printing,
February 1980.
Printed in the United
States of America.

To AMY
who always waited
for Mommy to
come home

FOREWORD

Joan Winmill Brown
and William F. Brown

I first met Meg in the lobby of a busy hotel.
My appointment with this beautiful, vibrant
young woman was supposed to last only an
hour. Four hours later we were still talking!
During that time, I sensed that she was a
woman God was going to use to help heal
hurts in countless lives. Meg had experienced
the most incredible heartaches in her young life
—a life that overcame, only to crumble again.
Then the miracle of Christ's love restored the
shattered pieces.

This story will break through many
man-made barriers of judgment that have been
built up over the years. It is a book I am so
thankful to see in print because we live in a
day when compassion is longed for by so
many.

Meg's story will sensitize hearts that have
become hardened to the tremendous needs

around them. It may shock some, but I applaud Tyndale House's decision to publish it and Meg's courage in being so honest.

Joan Winmill Brown
Author/actress

With seemingly no ballast for her soul, Meg Ashley moved through her life as haphazardly as an actor would run through a first reading of a play—but this was no rehearsal. She was wasting the only life she'd been given.

Then it happened. The change took place. The Man, Christ Jesus, came into her life and gave purpose for living where there had been only ashes and rubble. There wasn't room for both his beauty and the ugliness that she had borne for so long.

I first read Meg's story when she sent it to us in the form of a film script. It was well written, but crying out for the opportunity of being told in detail in a book. I urged her to rewrite it and she took my advice. I remember well the day Meg phoned excitedly to say Tyndale House had accepted it.

It is not easy for Meg to reach back into the agonies of her past, but she does it in order to help others who are still walking that lonely journey toward finding Christ.

Meg wanted to tell it—felt compelled to tell it—exactly as it all happened. I am glad she did. What hope it offers for others!

Bill Brown
President, World Wide Pictures

To my readers:

This story is true. God wrote it across the pages of my life. Some may say the story is full of coincidences that I have invested with more meaning than they deserve. I do not believe in chance, however. I believe in a God who has not finished breaking into time on behalf of his creation.

I do not understand why God dealt with me in the ways he did. I only know that the story unfolded chapter by chapter as I have recorded it.

The names of people and places have been changed to protect the children, and some characters have been condensed for the sake of clarity.

My prayer is that, as you read, you will

hunger for Jesus, and in hungering, search, and in searching, find him, embrace him, and begin a journey of your own.

Sincerely,

Meg Ashley

Victoria
Street

The time for stopping had come.

I had run from this time for years. I could run no more. Like an audience anticipating the rise of the curtain on the final scene of a play, I waited. Sitting in an old, stiff armchair in my little apartment on Victoria Street, I traced the mortar lines of the cinderblock wall before me, bracing myself for the onslaught of thoughts against which I had no defense, no place to hide.

I was twenty-three years old that September. I'd come to San Justin because I wanted to be near the ocean. The other coastal towns were too full of memories . . . this was the only place left to which I could escape.

My daughter Amy was nearly three years old. It is difficult to describe how much she meant to me by then. I know for certain that I would never have survived that terrible year after my divorce, had I not had her. But I was oblivious to her smiles and songs those days as the floodgates opened in my mind. I had a decision to make with three alternatives from which to choose. Each alternative carried something of death in it.

Months before, I had looked forward to a new marriage, a home for Amy. Chris and I had planned for the baby I now carried. But here I was, alone again, betrayed, five months pregnant. I was living on $250 a month. I had no real home to offer my children, no father. But more devastating than the circumstances that surrounded me was the fact that I had no hope.

"What are you going to do?" the voice demanded. "You can't put another baby through what you've put Amy through."

But how can I give up my child? I wondered. *How can I divorce myself from my own flesh?*

"You don't have to go on, you know," another voice, a dark one, whispered. "The ace . . . remember, *you* hold the ace. Use it now."

Suicide? I wondered as I watched Amy putting her dolly to bed in a shoe box filled with rags. *But what about Amy? I could never leave her!*

"Take her with you," that hideous dark voice suggested. "After all, is life really worth living? She'll only be destroyed, the same as you. She's better off dead."

Perhaps you're right, I thought, searching the cinderblock wall.

"Give the baby up, Meg," the other, the

clear voice said. "You made the mistakes that brought you here. Why should your baby pay for it the rest of his life? One of you will be crippled. You must choose whom that will be."

Oh, God, why can't I keep my baby? I cried out in silence as Amy flew into my arms.

"Why you crying, Mommy?" She started crying too. My outbursts of tears usually ended with us in each other's arms. I comforted her. I could not bear to see her cry.

"Let's go for a walk," I said, kissing her salty cheeks. "Let's go downtown!" I always tried to save fifty cents out of my unemployment check to spend on a treat each month. Our trip to the little cafe on Ave Del Rios to buy a cup of cocoa for her and coffee for me was the high spot of our weeks.

The only other intrusions into those days were the visits from Mr. McJames. He worked for the County Bureau of Adoptions. When Chris had turned Amy and me out into the street, I had driven in a burst of anger to the Bureau office in Santa Marta. Even as my fury subsided and I stood before the heavy glass door of the office, I had known this was one threshold I had to cross. My first talk with Mr. McJames had helped, somehow. He was a young man, not much older than I, and he had listened as I told why I'd come. I always felt he had wanted to comfort me that day. The most he'd been able to offer was a box of tissues.

I looked forward to his visits to my apartment. He always came with forms to fill out, questions to ask. What kind of family did I come from?

I answered with a mixture of feelings. "They're a good family," I told him, and my admission condemned me. "We were never rich, but never poor either. My mother owns a dress shop." I went on to brag about the successes of my brother and sister. My dad was hard to explain. He and I hadn't communicated in years. He and Mom had divorced a few years before and each had remarried. I wasn't even certain where Dad was now.

"Well, what sort of education did you have?" Mr. McJames asked as he wrote quickly.

My thoughts rose in defense. "I was an honor student at Marshall College. In fact, I was awarded two full scholarships. I had to turn one of them down. I only stayed three semesters. They didn't have any more answers for life than I did, so I left."

"Answers for life?" Mr. McJames stopped writing. I wondered if there was a space on the form for such information.

I was hard put to find the words to explain what I meant. "I know," I blurted out. "Wait a minute!" I went to the bedroom and rummaged through my drawers until I found the plastic zipper case in which I'd been stuffing my writing for the past four years. Finding the piece I wanted, I thrust it into his hands. I didn't care if he thought I was crazy, as long as he understood.

He read slowly out loud,

There is a surging chaos in me
That is, perhaps, the memory
Of energy in motion
For the first time.

Back in my darkness
A constant reliving
Of the first glimpse
Of light.

Out of the silence
Of my aloneness, a response
Of joy to the first strains
Of harmony.

He reread it to himself, his lips moving.

"Well," I asked him as he looked up at me. "Don't you see?" He sat looking at the sheet of paper in his hands. "I mean, look at me!" My cotton maternity dress hid nothing of my already bulging figure. "Look what I've come to . . . and that!" I pointed at the poem. "Something doesn't add up . . . something is missing, don't you think?

"I've believed since I was a little girl that there was a beautiful secret about life. In fact, I can remember a night back on our farm in Wisconsin, looking out the dining room window into the backyard. It was winter. The snow was silvery blue in the moonlight. I knew, I knew as I looked out that window that there was something or someone out there waiting for me to find it or him or whatever it was. I've been looking ever since." I paused to catch my breath and to search his face for understanding.

"I promised I would grow up as fast as I could so I could go find it. I believed that when I grew up, I'd discover the secret." I laughed at the irony of the memory. "My folks never could understand why I was always in such a hurry to grow up." Thinking back was painful; I was grown up now and was no closer to knowing the answer than I had been then.

"Do you know the secret?" I whispered.

Mr. McJames was not writing anymore. He stared at the form in his hands. The silence hurt him.

Why do I bother? I thought. *No one knows.*

I spoke to break the hanging question. "When will you be back?"

"About two weeks," he answered as he put away his papers. "What did you say was your due date?"

"Christmas time." The dull knife twisted slightly. "My due date is Christmas day."

After he was gone, the battle began again.

"What are you going to do?" the clear voice asked, relentlessly.

I want my baby! everything within me screamed.

"End it all. Kill yourself, the baby, and Amy!" the dark voice demanded. "You're a fool! There are no answers. You'll find no meaning. Give up!"

The darkness that swirled around me for those six weeks should have driven me mad. There was only one glimmer of light breaking into my days. It was a tree. Outside my bathroom window stood a small eucalyptus tree. The main trunk grew up into three main sections, each one carrying a weight of smaller branches and leaves.

I liked my bathroom the best of all the rooms in that apartment. It was white. The other rooms were dark; the living room was chartreuse! I could always escape to the bathroom. Even Amy left me alone in there. I loved to take long baths and look at my tree. If Amy peeked in and caught me crying, it was easy to say the wetness on my face and redness of my eyes came from scrubbing. I wanted so badly to be clean.

I loved that tree. Always when I would look at the three main branches swaying in the breeze, the thought would come, "Father, Son, and Holy Ghost."

Funny, I thought. *They are so far away.*

The pressure of the darkness subsided when, after six weeks of struggle, I finally silenced the dark voice in me.

I addressed it: *I will try one more time. I'll go one more round. If I fail again, that will be it. You can have me, my baby, and Amy.* Thus I made a pact with Death and all the powers behind it. Once that was settled, it was easier to face the other question.

"You know you do not have to sign the final papers until eight weeks after your baby is born, don't you?" Mr. McJames asked one afternoon.

I understood.

"We will not pressure you to make a decision for or against adoption. But you must understand that once you've signed those papers, that's it. You'll have no rights to your child, ever again. You'll have no contact with him or with his adoptive parents."

I gulped the pain down and nodded.

"You'll need to sign some papers before then to allow us to take your baby from the hospital and place him in a foster home. It may take some time to place him permanently." He rose to leave and started to speak again. All he could do was stand there looking down at me. He cleared his throat and left without a word.

I put Amy to bed early those days. Time hung heavy on my hands.

The quiet voice demanded over and over, "What are you going to do? Whom do you choose to suffer? You can give your child a good chance in life if you give him up. Look at Amy!"

I could scarcely bear to look at Amy. She was too beautiful, too sensitive, too loving.

Sleep never came easily. The questioning never stopped. I would go to bed at 5:30 P.M. because there was nothing else to do and the oblivion of sleep was the closest thing to death I could find. There was escape in unconsciousness. But as though taunted by a demon, I searched for sleep in vain. Lying on my back was the only comfortable position I could find. My head ached constantly as though a steel band was tightening around my skull. I had to find release.

Our Father, I gasped, thinking of my tree, *who art in heaven.* I pulled the prayer back through the forgotten corridor of years. *Hallowed be thy name.* What came next? I could not remember.

Forgive us our debts as we forgive our debtors . . . and lead us not into temptation . . . for thine is the glory and the power forever. Amen.

Quiet. For a moment. Then the voice began to question me again.

Our Father, I retaliated. *Who art in heaven. Hallowed be thy name.* I shot out the words like bullets. *Thy will be done, thy kingdom come, on earth as it is in heaven.*

So on and on, hour after hour, I fought for peace of mind. Eventually sleep would come.

Praying what I could remember of the Lord's Prayer became my only defense. Night after night, over and over, those words ushered me into quietness.

Then it happened . . . as gently as a drop of rain touching a forest meadow. He spoke.

"Meg." I knew he was calling me. "I want you to go to church tomorrow."

Yes, God, I answered simply. *But where?*

I saw in my mind an image of a church building, as clearly as if I were looking at a picture postcard.

OK, I responded, *I'll go. It might be a Jewish synagogue for all I know, but I'll go.*

Sleep came quickly that night.

Sunday morning dawned sunny and clear. I dressed Amy in her prettiest dress. I chose an expensive beige gown for myself, a reminder of days when I had moved in fashionable circles, on the arm of rich and cultured companions. The dress was elastic enough to accommodate my bulging figure. For some reason, I wanted to be beautiful that day.

We drove downtown. I was shaking my head at myself. I didn't even know where I was going at 9:00 A.M.! And church services didn't start until 11 A.M., from what I could remember.

Then, looking up a side street, I saw the church. It was just as I had seen it the night before. I read the sign: San Justin Presbyterian Church. I was relieved to be on somewhat familiar ground. Then I noticed that there was a 9:30 A.M. service.

That's nice, I thought, *we're right on time!*

I took Amy to the Sunday school room marked for her age. She protested being left there, but for once I knew it was best. Entering the sanctuary was a strange experience. I hadn't been inside a church since I'd left home more than seven years ago. An elderly woman made room for me in her pew and shared her hymnal.

The music and the words echoed deep within me, bringing me back to when I was a child, when I had sung the same words:

A mighty fortress is our God
A bulwark never failing. . . .

I felt a warmth in that sanctuary a little like one feels when going home.

It was Worldwide Communion Sunday. I wondered at it as I read the bulletin and noticed the table set at the front of the church.

Communion . . . I haven't had communion in seven years! You called me back for communion! I bowed my head in amazement.

As my gaze wandered around the sanctuary, I was caught and held by the scene depicted in one of the stained glass windows. It showed Christ at Gethsemane. The agony of that Man!

Oh, God, I whispered, *if he could go through that, I can go through this!*

Hope was born . . . hope that, somehow, I would come through.

Week after week I returned to that church, to that window. Amy soon looked forward to her Sunday school class with excitement. It provided her an opportunity to play with other children, something our life style had never included. I sat in the same pew week after week, absorbing the peace, watching the window, hearing the words spoken, the songs sung. I spoke to no one. A young woman approached me once with overtures of friendliness. My fear of being known and once again rejected turned my response to ice. I was not approached again.

Months passed. I grew larger and larger. I was too small to carry so large a baby. My obstetrician, Dr. Leeds, was concerned. Soon walking was so painful it brought tears to my eyes.

The Christmas season approached. The city crews put up the decorations. Carols could be heard playing in the busy shops. My older brother, Les, home on leave from the Navy, came to see me. Les loved me. He always had, in his quiet way. He slept on the floor and said nothing of the events that had brought me to this place. He knew, as did my mother, that I was considering giving this baby up for adoption. My life style had gone against everything my mother had taught me. Later she confessed how she had prayed year after year.

"God didn't hear me!" she cried. "He didn't help you! You just got worse and worse and worse!"

When faced with the shame of having an illegitimate grandchild, she had told me not to come home anymore if I kept the child. Under no conditions was I to come home during the pregnancy.

I had put her through hell, the way I'd lived. I could not blame her for her words, even though it made my decision so much more difficult.

I didn't have a Christmas tree that year. My home was bare of decoration. On Christmas Eve Les bundled Amy and me up and took us for a ride up the coast to see the Christmas lights. That was the first year of the energy crisis. People didn't have their homes lit up as in years past.

Dark, I thought, *just like me.*

Les waited around until December 27. The baby did not come. Finally he decided to go to Mom's place four hours away for the rest of his leave. I packed a suitcase for Amy. She might as well have a Christmas, even if I couldn't.

When they were gone I walked slowly downtown. I missed Amy skipping along beside me. I went back home to wait. The day passed without a word being spoken.

The next day I walked to my doctor's appointment. It was beautiful and warm outside. I knew I looked a sight. My maternity dress hiked up in the front. I guess maternity dresses weren't made big enough to span such a girth as mine.

Dr. Leeds treated me gently, as he had all along. That I was a "Medi-cal" patient did not minimize his service. I usually broke down during my examinations. It was one time I could not escape the reality of the life that was within me.

Dr. Leeds called me into his office after he'd checked me. He looked pensive as I waited for him to speak.

"How soon can you get to the hospital?" he asked.

"Why, I could be there in half an hour, I guess. Is something wrong?"

He made a telephone call to the OB ward of the Community Hospital. I didn't understand much of what he said, except that I was expected to be there by noon.

"The baby is in danger, Meg," he spoke as he hung up the phone. "We can't have you out walking around. We've got to have you where we can help you quickly."

I breathed in slowly. "OK, I'll get there right away."

"I'll meet you there in less than an hour," he assured me and I walked out deep in thought.

I didn't dare let him know I had to walk home. I didn't feel in any danger and the day was so beautiful. I savored every step, every moment. I drew in all the warmth the sun would offer, knowing the storm was soon to break.

The taxi driver dropped me off at the front door of the hospital with relief. I clung nervously to my overnight case and admitted myself at the desk. As the large swinging doors to the maternity ward closed behind me I felt as though a coffin lid was being nailed shut over my head. I knew I'd not leave there the same.

Twenty hours later, after a long and difficult labor, I delivered a ten-pound boy. He was beautiful. I was very weak and having nervous convulsions, so a nurse wrapped me snugly in heated blankets. I was taken to a dark, empty room and there I sank into an oblivion deeper than sleep.

Later I was taken to a room where I could recuperate alone. The doctor's forms must have indicated my intention to relinquish my baby, for the nurses were careful not to refer to the fact that I'd just been through childbirth. I was treated, for the most part, as though I was merely recovering from a serious operation. Their intent was kindness, I knew, but it was difficult to refrain from screaming the truth at them. The next day, December 31, I called for the nurse.

"I'd like to see my baby now," I stated.

Her eyes widened. "Are you sure you want to do that? I mean, well, most of the girls who . . . who, well, most of them don't want to see their babies." She could hardly believe my request.

"Ma'am," I stared hard at her. "He is *my* son. I want to see him."

"All right," she turned in a huff, "suit yourself."

My bed was next to the window and looked out on a small, grassy area. There was a young tree planted in the center. Under the wind that had risen, the sapling was being lashed severely.

The nurse came in quickly and placed a neatly wrapped bundle of blankets in my arms. She drew a curtain, giving me privacy.

I was afraid to open the blankets that moved so gently in my arms. I stared out at the tormented sapling and uttered a low cry.

It had to be done. I knew I had to hold my son, look at him, trace the lines of his face, etch the memory of him deep into my mind. The only desire I would not give in to was the yearning to tear aside my gown and put the tiny babe to my breast. I knew if I did that, I would never let him go.

But the rest, the rest I had to do. I had to make my decision as difficult as I possibly could. Then, if I could still give him away, I would never wonder, in the years to come, if the decision were made from all of me. If I could not see him, hold him, and still relinquish him, then I must not give him up, for surely the years would crush me.

I pulled the blanket aside.

"Hello," I whispered. His eyes were dark, deep blue. He was surprisingly alert. I was glad I had been able to deliver him without medication.

"I love you." I touched his little hand and he grabbed my finger tightly. "You know that, don't you . . . that I love you?" My visi⌐n began to blur. "They'll tell you that, I think, that I loved you. That's why I gave you up, because I loved you." I hugged him close and buried my face to sob into his blankets.

Oh, God! I screamed out in my soul. *Oh, God! The pain!* I, who had not cried out once through all the hours of labor, now faced a far greater tearing.

I gasped for breath. All the months of waiting, of fighting back the storm, ended as the pain in my chest made breathing nearly impossible. I fought for air, lowering the infant to the crook of my arm. The torrent of rain sheeting down my window eased the viselike grip on my heart. I turned back to look at my boy. Still he seemed to watch me.

Silently then, I touched his nose, his eyes, ran my finger across his brow and down his cheeks. I touched his lips. He, thinking only of life, tried to suck on my finger. I let him have my knuckle. He tried so furiously to draw nourishment from it that I had to laugh.

But the sound of my laughter was like a slap across my face. I began to moan and the

moaning struggled to be released into a scream
. . . a scream that would never end. The madness rose within me and I knew if I let it go, the screaming would go on and on until I was safe within the confines of insanity. I fought the rising fury and beat it down. Quickly I rang for the nurse. Quickly she appeared.

"Take him back," I croaked. "I do not want to see him again."

Havoc must have been written across my face, for the nurse said nothing as she turned away. I could not watch them leave. I saw only the tree outside my window. The storm had risen in ferocity. The tree was being beaten unmercifully. How could God let such a thing go on and on and on!

God! I screamed out at the storm. *God, I can't stand this! I can't stand any more pain. . . . You've got to give me something for this pain!*

God, and the final scene drew to a close, *if you are there, if you are even real, I have to know . . . NOW!* I gasped for control. *I can't go through any more months or years not knowing. If you are there, I have to know.* I could not search anymore. I laid all my cards on the table.

The silence was full. Then he spoke to me again . . . just as he had months before. I wondered in a flash if that inner voice had been prodding me all my life, but had fallen on deaf ears. The voice was so familiar, as though it belonged to Someone I had always known.

"Meg, you're going to live the rest of your life one day at a time. If you try to carry any more than that it will destroy you. Sufficient unto the day is the evil thereof."

I turned angrily from the window. I wanted the pain to go away. He only told me how to bear it. I wanted the storm to stop. God wanted the roots to dig deeper into the soil.

There was no other way out. Because I saw I had no alternative, I resolved to live one day at a time. As my mind wandered ahead to times when my arms would hang empty at my side, when my breasts would ache in their fullness, when my heart would be silent from all song, I pulled back into the present. I bound my thoughts to the day I was in, and then I could breathe.

The nurses heard me crying and brought me sedatives. I took everything they offered.

On January 2 I was released. Les came to take me to my mother's to heal. The nurse got me seated in the wheelchair over my protests. As we approached the nursery, I made her stop. She watched as I walked stiffly to the window looking over the bassinets. There he was. I could spot him in a second. I reached out to touch him, but the glass got in my way. How long I stood there, clawing the glass, tears streaming down my cheeks, I do not know.

"Goodbye," I whispered, "goodbye. . . ."

The nurse, weeping herself, grabbed me brusquely by the shoulders. "Just go," she shouted as she pushed me back into the wheelchair. "Just go . . . it'll be so much easier if you just go!" Pushing me fiercely, she rushed out into the lobby. The heavy swinging doors thudded shut behind me.

To Know
the Sea

I returned to San Justin the first week in
February feeling like an opera house after all
the people have gone home . . . quiet and
echoingly empty. Little did I know the wooing
had begun.

My first Sunday home found me sitting
deathlike in my pew, wondering about the
Man in the window. The church service was
going on around me when he broke into my
thoughts again.

"Meg, I want you to go to the adult class
today."

OK, God. I found the announcement printed
in the bulletin.

After the service I approached three people
who were conversing and asked for the class. I
had seen the woman in the group before. She
had tried to be friendly to me once.

Darrell Myers was the Youth Pastor. He was

a husky, handsome man about my age. He had a look about him I had always associated with "professional Christianity." I wondered if there was anything real behind it.

All week Darrell had anticipated hearing the guest pastor speak in one of the two morning services.

"There is no adult class today," he spoke. He hesitated.

Drop it, he was thinking to himself, wanting to ignore, for once, the tugging he felt at his will. But his will had long ago been yielded to Another. So Darrell spoke again.

"But I'd be willing to teach a class for you if you'd like. You'd be the only one there."

"Yes," I said. "I'd like to talk to someone."

Darrell turned and led me to his office, the longed-for sermon put behind him, and began the gentle process of midwifing in a spiritual birth.

We talked. He tenderly touched me with his questions until he found where I was yet alive. He asked about my children. I could be philosophical about anything else, but not about them. When he had touched the nerve, he backed off and began to pray for this stranger who had come.

"Tell me what you know about God," he said.

I was relieved to have the conversation turn to less sensitive ground.

"Why, God is energy!" I replied. How could he be anything else? There is no other evidence.

"But, say," I thought it my turn to prod, "if God is God, doesn't need anything . . . is omniscient and all that, then why Jesus?"

I've got him! I thought. *There is the flaw in the story! How could Jesus, with all his suffering, possibly be God? What did he have to prove? How could God be God and still need to go through all that? A sure victory,* I gloated. *He has no answer.*

A sure victory, indeed.

Darrell's prayers had cleared the road. He spoke the answer quietly, realizing fully what hung in the balance.

"God didn't need to send Jesus, Meg. *You* needed him to be sent."

The Bible says that when Jesus comes for his people, we will be changed in the twinkling of an eye.

So it was that quiet February morning. He came to me through Darrell's simple explanation of the truth, and in a twinkling of an eye, I was changed. I knew who the Man was at Gethsemane, why he'd come, and why he'd died. He had come to die for me.

The pieces of the puzzle snapped into place. The dark corridors in my mind were inundated with light. Every door flew open before the baptism of reality I had just received. In a sense, time stopped; eternity began. I sat there as though stunned.

"Would you like to pray?" Darrell asked softly.

"Why, yes, of course." I realized I needed to respond to all that had just happened.

I followed Darrell in prayer from rebellion to repentance and from repentance into the family of the King. A new kind of tears washed out my eyes. I had never cried for joy in all my life.

Darrell was smiling as he led me to the door.

"If you could find one word to describe how you feel right now, what would it be?" he asked curiously.

It took me only a moment to know. "Whole." I was amazed at the answer myself. "For the first time in my life I feel whole!"

"If you were to look back at the meaning of the word 'to be saved' that's in the New Testament, you'd find that 'to be made whole' is one of the ways to translate it," Darrell went on, walking outside with me.

I pondered his words. "To be saved . . . to be made whole. . . ." What had always before been some vague doctrine finally made sense.

The man and woman Darrell had left an hour before were still standing outside the building. I wondered if they had been praying.

"I'd like you to meet a new sister in the Lord," Darrell said to them. "Meg Tarken, meet John and Joanne Sumners."

I did not understand why they were so happy, but I was suddenly shy of their friendship. I wanted to go home and try to understand all that had happened. I knew I had become a Christian, and I chuckled at the thought. I had always despised those people; now I was one of them. Meeting the Man behind the name, the Christ, made all the difference.

Even my apartment seemed peaceful as we entered the quiet rooms. Amy, caught in the happiness of the moment, was singing little songs she'd learned in Sunday school.

"Jesus lubs me, dis I know. For da Bibue tells me so."

Oh, how far back you reach, Lord! I marveled, remembering a dark-haired girl who'd sung that same song years before.

"So you were the one who called to me!" I whispered as I saw again that winter night fraught with promise. "So I was right . . . all those years, there was Someone to find."

How long, I wondered, *before I understand you?*

"It will take you the rest of your life," came the quiet, happy answer.

My closet door stood open and I saw things there I did not want to see . . . dresses that said things about me that were no longer true. I tore them off their hangers and took them to the garbage bin outside. Though I had only four dresses and a coat left, I felt like a queen.

Then the little brown box had to be considered. I had kept illegal drugs hidden in it for years.

I don't think I need this stuff anymore, I mused, looking over the supply. I didn't know much about the God I now served, but the sense of cleanness was so delicious, I wanted nothing to spoil it. The toilet served as a useful disposal.

Never again would I be afraid to look a policeman in the eye or to answer a knock at the door.

As Amy slept, I cleaned my house—vacuumed, dusted, scrubbed, and polished. When she awoke, we walked to the beach.

The ocean had always frightened me. Though I was drawn to its beauty and the relentlessness of its surf, I had always felt threatened. It was as though the ocean had something to say I did not want to hear.

That afternoon I understood its message at last. Wordlessly it sang a love song to its Creator; praise was the recurring theme of all its sound, its beauty, its power. I was amazed. What had been my enemy was now my friend. I realized the change had come in me. I had come home.

Dark
Until
Easter

Within the next two weeks three more big changes had come. I attended my first Christian fellowship meeting, I found a job, and I signed the final release papers on my son.

Darrell's wife, Sandra, called on me the Tuesday after my conversion. She was tall and beautiful, so totally different from my stereotype of a Christian woman. Her long dark hair reflected the light as she sat in my living room keeping a watchful eye on her lively son. Brad and Amy became fast friends.

"You are my sister now, Meg," Sandra explained. "We'd like to include you in some of the things we do." Her eyes sparkled. I was not afraid to meet them, for only love and acceptance shone there.

"Friday nights we get together in people's homes to worship and share. Would you like to come with us this Friday? You could use our baby-sitter for Amy."

"Why, yes, I'd like that," I replied shyly. Except for Mr. McJames and Les, Sandra and her son were the only visitors I'd had in my home.

I hardly knew how to dress to go to a fellowship gathering. I chose a long black velour gown that had a more modest cut than the ones I'd discarded.

What a contrast the meeting was to any other I had known! I was used to darkened rooms filled with smoke and throbbing music. These people met in a bright living room that bubbled with laughter and song. About seventy people—high school and college students and middle-aged couples—sat casually about, sharing from the Bible and relating the Scriptures to their lives. Their uninhibited joy was hard to take at first. When they sang they clapped their hands or raised their arms. Some even cried unashamedly. My cool front was no defense against the warmth I was encountering.

Late in the evening Sandra introduced me around. I had only one Scripture verse I could share and I didn't even know where it was found. "Be still and know that I am God." From there I laid before these beloved strangers the story of how God had brought me to a place of stillness and how, through the relinquishing of my son, I had found the Son of God. They cried with me and then united to pray for my baby. They claimed a Christian home for him and went on to ask for a job for me.

As we were leaving, Sandra put a bulging envelope in my hands.

"What's this?" I asked, startled.

"A love gift," she replied, smiling.

"I can't take this!" I exclaimed, pushing the envelope back into her hands. "What do they take me for?"

"They love you," she assured me gently, wrapping my hands around the envelope. "I don't know who thought of it, but I do believe the Lord wants you to have it."

I gulped down the emotion that surged in my throat.

"You're part of a family now, Meg. Nothing will ever be the same again."

I lost the battle for composure and wiped away tear after tear as we walked out into the cool, starry night. I drank in big gulps of the salty air and searched hard in the sky. The love that repentance had sparked now burst into a flickering flame.

"Well," Sandra began later as we sat in their driveway, "aren't you going to count it?"

So there in the dark I dumped the contents of the envelope onto my lap. Nearly $67.00, more than enough to get Amy and me through the coming weeks.

The week after my conversion I had also gone job hunting. Though I hated the thought of going back to waitressing, I applied to several restaurants. I'd never go back to working in bars or fancy cocktail lounges again. I drew that line. But still I prayed for something else.

The Thursday before my first fellowship meeting I went up the freeway to the state college and applied for a secretarial job. The next night, after the fellowship had prayed, I still had no answer.

The following Monday morning, the placement office of the college called. I could begin work the next week.

The next day, Tuesday, I appeared in Santa Marta to sign away all rights to my son. I stipulated then to the agency that my son was to go into a Christian home. They had tentatively placed him in a home in which the woman was Mormon and the husband a Lutheran. I wielded what little power I had to stop that placement before I signed the relinquishment. The fact that the home was divided in its beliefs was enough to make me say "No."

Six weeks later Mr. McJames called to say my son had gone to an evangelical Christian family in northern California. I gave my approval to the placement and the file closed. I had given my son a home.

It was Amy who reassured me that my decision for my boy had been right. At 7 A.M. every morning I would walk her down to the preschool on the corner.

"Mommy, can I go to work with you today?"

"No, dear, there is no place there for children."

"I'll be quiet." Her blue eyes pleaded her sincerity.

"Oh, honey," I stopped to lift her up and walked on with her arms tight around my neck. "I'll be back pretty soon."

"Before lunch?"

"No, but before supper."

"Mommy, I want to go with you!"

Day after day I'd have to become firm, almost harsh, as I'd insist she stay.

She learned not to cry, but the sight of her standing inside the door gulping down her tears was even harder to take. When I would pick her up at 6 P.M. she'd not cry either. She would cling to me, wordlessly, all the way home. I wondered how long we could stand it.

Perhaps if this was the first time I'd had to leave her I could have shrugged off her sadness as something she would have to outgrow. But I had been leaving her since she was nine months old, since the summer of 1970 when my marriage to Randy had begun to fall apart. Two years after the divorce, my hopes for a new marriage had proven false, and I was left pregnant; only then did I stay home with Amy. There was not much call for a pregnant cocktail waitress, and I was tired, too tired to fight anymore. Those six months of having Mommy home were like heaven to a three-year-old. She knew then what she'd been missing before. It made my leaving now tantamount to desertion.

God, I'd speak aloud to him as I sped down the freeway, *she needs a daddy.*

The fellowship meetings helped in a way, but at the same time accentuated the problem.

I was the only divorcée in the group; Amy, the only fatherless child. Some of the married couples tried to bring us into their family circles, but there was always a time to say "Good-night" and I would carry Amy, asleep in my arms, into our empty house. Then I would crawl into bed and fight the cold. The physical intimacy of marriage was not missed nearly as much as the companionship, the long talks in the middle of the night, having someone there.

If I had not had Amy I could have ignored my own feelings more easily. But she was always there. Many a morning I'd find her nestled in my bed and we would begin again.

"Mommy, how come you hafta go to work?"

"I have to earn money so we can live, sweetheart."

"I don't need any money."

"Yes, but you need food and we have to pay money to live here."

"Let's go to the bank and get some and you stay home today!" Amy would plead with all her innocent wiles as we walked the plank down to preschool.

"Goodbye, darling. See you tonight," and I'd hug her gently.

"Bye, Mama," she'd whisper and stand there watching as I closed the door.

Oh, God! I'd cry again and again. *How long?* No answer came.

Steve and Marsha Rogers took a special interest in Amy and me. Prior to their marriage, they had both been divorced. Somehow they had coped with the scars and together had built a happy marriage. I was often invited to go on family outings with them. Early in March they asked if I would accompany them to a weekend retreat in the desert. Several high school and college students were also coming. It promised to be a time of laughter and prayer. Steve and Marsha also hoped it would be a time of spiritual renewal in the lives of some of the youth who would attend.

Amy was excited to go and, of course, fell asleep in the car after the first hour of travel. I was not so peaceful, for also invited on this trip was a young man I'd noticed at the fellowship meetings. Jake was a new Christian too. His background made me feel like I'd come out of a convent. He had been a high priest in the occult—Satan worship. The damage still showed. He fought relentless battles . . . exhaustion was evident in his face, in his eyes. Yet his insights into the Bible impressed me and he understood very well the seriousness of spiritual warfare.

The weekend was even more than Steve and Marsha had hoped it would be. The Holy Spirit was evident as he convicted, comforted, and empowered life after life. Between meetings and play times, with the sage and the moonlight setting the scene, Jake and I began to love. Our talks came slowly. Our prayers at first were full of fear and hope together. Jake understood the echo in my heart, for he too ached for a voice to answer his. Did I dare to hope God had answered my prayers so soon? Was this the man?

Questions whirled through my mind all the way home. I had to be sure. I had to know if this was indeed God's will for me.

Show me, Lord, help me, I entreated day after day as I drove to work.

Jake and I began attending fellowship meetings together. Though the courtship was noted by everyone, no one spoke of it. Some of my new friends seemed happy. Steve and Marsha Rogers were thrilled. Others, like Darrell and Sandra Myers, were hesitant, worried.

One weekend when I shared with Sandra about Jake's talk of marriage, she finally blurted out, "Don't you think this is happening too fast, Meg?"

She saw the walls go up and hastened to add, "You're both so new in the Lord. There's so much healing to be done. Can't you wait?"

"That's easy advice to give," I retorted. "You have everything, Darrell, a home . . . you've never had to scrounge day after day to make ends meet!"

Her head bowed beneath the truth I hurled at her.

"Yes, Meg, but I know Jesus, and he has promised to be sufficient for you."

"Tell that to Amy tomorrow morning!" I slammed back. "See if it makes any difference to her!"

Sandra put her arms around me and groaned

softly. I had hurt her and I was ashamed.

"I'm sorry," I sniffed. "It's just that it's so hard, every day. We've prayed, Sandra, really we have. We want God's will for our lives. Can't you believe he'll show us? Why does this have to be wrong?"

She had no answers, but promised to pray . . . not a glib promise for her, for she began an assault of intercession that very day.

Meanwhile Jake spent more and more time at my apartment. He worked nights but was through by 6 A.M. Often he would come by to have breakfast with us before I hurried off to work.

The first week of April Jake proposed and I accepted. May 6 was set to be the wedding day. I gave notice at work to terminate the end of April and wrote home to tell the happy news. Then my evenings were filled with plans and sewing. I designed and made my wedding dress. It hung outside my closet, shimmering white in the darkness—a mute reminder of the purity Christ had purchased for me.

We sent one hundred and fifty invitations and excitedly opened the gifts that came. I wished only that the cold stone in my heart would dissolve. . . .

"Meg," Jake began one quiet evening after Amy had gone to bed. "Meg," and he traced the veins down the back of my hand, "I really believe God has led us to this."

The cold knot tightened slightly. "Why, yes, so do I," I replied.

"You know, in God's eyes we're already

married," Jake stated simply. "I wonder why we have to wait for some stupid paper to be filed away somewhere."

That's a new line! some cynical voice within me cried.

Wait, I answered it, *listen to what he has to say.*

"I don't know," I stammered, trying hard to remember Bible verses about engagement.

"Well, in Jesus' time, after the promises were made, couples were essentially married," Jake went on. "And we're promised to each other, aren't we?"

"Y-yes," I stammered, frightened now.

Jake sensed the fear and backed off. But the subject came up again and again. Finally I went to a couple in the fellowship.

"What about it?" I asked them. "Is it OK or isn't it?"

The fellow looked me right in the eye. "Well, if the couple is really committed to one another and marriage is imminent, yes, I believe it is OK. Of course, if they can't handle it, they'd better wait."

His wife concurred.

I had little defense left after that and I wasn't sure I needed any. Maybe I was being silly . . . maybe they right. The night came when I didn't say "No" anymore.

I couldn't look at the dress on the closet after he'd gone. I dragged through the next day feeling more alone than I'd felt in a long, long time. After the next night I couldn't stand it.

"Jake . . . I can't go on like this!"

He turned slowly where he sat on the side of the couch, tying his shoes.

"I mean, the dress . . . how can I honestly wear that dress when . . . when all this has gone on before?"

"Oh, come on!" he exclaimed, disgusted. "What's the difference? You were hardly a virgin before I came along."

He rose to his feet, leaving me reeling under his blow.

"Oh, Jake," I cried, "I love you, really I do!" I wrapped the quilt tightly around me and followed him across the living room. "But Jesus made me clean! It's not just a story, it can't be just a story!"

Jake turned at the door and held me gently.

"It's OK," he reassured me, smoothing my ruffled hair. "What difference does a few weeks make? If it's so right afterward, how can it be so wrong now?"

"I don't know," I sobbed. "I don't know . . . only I can't stand it! No more, Jake," I looked at him fiercely. "No more, we'll wait. I don't know why, it just isn't right this way."

"OK," he dropped his arms, and shrugged coldly. "Anything you say. Good-night." The door closed after him.

I do not know how long I stood there in the darkened room, but I ended up sobbing on the floor. The sense of cleanness I had cherished was gone.

"Oh, God! What have I done?" Such actions before I'd met Christ had caused me no shame.

Now they took on a terrible significance. "How can you ever forgive me?"

Jake did not come by so often as before and when he did he was cool and distant. I put the wedding gown in the back of my closet. I could not bear the reproach of its whiteness.

Easter was coming, and with it, communion service. The pastor urged his congregation to search their hearts for unconfessed sin, encouraging us to prepare for the Lord's Table. I didn't have to search very hard. I was haunted by my sin. The sparkle had left my eyes, a fact I tried to hide. I did not know if God would or even could forgive me, a Christian, of so gross a sin . . . but I had to ask. I had no choice but to ask.

I went to the church early Easter morning. The fog had not yet lifted. I stood out in the patio, hesitating to enter the sanctuary. There, watching the sun fight through the clouds, I went before the Father. All I could do was confess what he already knew and ask for the forgiveness that cost him so much. I waited there, wanting him to speak. But he had already spoken and his words came back to assure me of his love:

"If we confess our sins, he is faithful and just to forgive us our sins, and to cleanse us from all unrighteousness."

. . . *and to cleanse us from all unrighteousness.* I knew it was done. I was clean again. *Never again,* I vowed, watching the sunlight stream through the clouds, *never again will I cause you such sorrow.*

I entered the sanctuary alone, beginning to understand the Man in the window, seeing more clearly than ever before what "grace" was all about. With a new reverence I took the bread and drank from the cup before me.

Eternity
at a
Stoplight

Wedding plans accelerated as May approached. I resigned from my job at the college at the end of April and moved out of my apartment. The Sumners had a spare bedroom in their spacious home they kept available to people who needed a place to stay. This was part of their ministry, and I did not hesitate to ask if Amy and I could stay there the six days before the wedding. They were quick to welcome us. We stored Amy's crib in their garage. For the first time she had a "big-girl bed," one she shared with the Sumners' seven-year-old daughter.

On May 3 I was sitting at Joanne's kitchen table busily assembling my sister's bridesmaid dress. Joanne sat opposite me, watching and chatting as she sipped her coffee.

I sighed. "I can't figure out why I feel so afraid," I confessed, and then gave a little laugh. "It doesn't make sense somehow that I should be so scared."

Joanne's cup went down with a clink.

"What do you mean?" she prodded.

"Oh, I don't know," I answered, absorbed in the hem of the sleeve before me. "I just hope the Lord takes away this horrible feeling before I have to walk down the aisle."

Jake came then and we went out to lunch, leaving Joanne sobered and full of thought. She went slowly to the phone and made some calls. As Jake and I were coming up the walk an hour later, Joanne and John were just leaving.

Joanne hesitated, then said, "We're going to Darrell's house to pray. Would you like to come?"

"Yes!" I blurted out, everything inside me agreeing.

Jake was disgruntled. Later when he saw the cars parked outside Darrell's driveway, he muttered, "Looks like they're ganging up on us."

"Don't be silly," I said. "Come on!" I didn't understand why he dragged his feet so. Why shouldn't we pray for guidance as we had all along?

Four couples were there: Darrell and Sandra Myers, Steve and Marsha Rogers, John and Joanne Sumners, and Bill and Marilyn Schoberg. The Schobergs were an older couple. Bill was the adult Sunday school teacher at the church, the one who'd been ill the day of my conversion. He began to ask Jake some questions while Jake sat alone before the cold fireplace answering as little as he could. I was surprised by his resistance. These people were our friends!

Joanne shared how my confession of fear had thrown a spark into the kindling of worry she felt for us. After talking with the others, none of whom had wanted to meddle, she'd discovered the same concern in all of them. We began to pray. What was wrong? I did not know.

Suddenly, I felt as though I'd been slapped across the face. My eyes flew open. I saw Jake sitting on the hearth, shrouded in darkness. In all our courtship he had shared very little about the occult. The information was dangerous, for it gave Satan a weapon to use against the knower. What little Jake did share stayed with me for years. But in that moment I saw evil all around Jake and I cried out, "No! No! Don't do it! Don't!"

The quiet prayers around me ended in a jolt as the others stared, shocked, at me—then at Jake. He answered their unspoken questions.

"If I can't have Meg, I don't want Jesus either!" The significance of his words stunned us all. I felt a dagger sink deep within me, yet at the same time I felt relief as the stone of fear disappeared.

Bill, John, and the others rushed in to countermand Jake's statement. Surely he didn't mean what he'd said!

But he did mean it. I turned quietly to Joanne. "I want to go home."

As I rose to leave I caught my breath and

said, "I don't see how we can go on. There are too many problems, too much to work out. I think we'd better wait to get married." I searched for Jake's eyes, but he refused to meet my glance. I turned pleadingly to Joanne. She understood my desire to escape and walked with me to the door.

Later that night John returned, discouraged by Jake's refusal to reason with them. Jake admitted that at the moment I'd called out, he'd been calling on Satan to come and destroy the people praying there. Bill Schoberg had stopped John as he was leaving to go home and asked if he was prepared for the spiritual warfare that could come. John shared with us what his answer had been. "Greater is he that is within us than he that is in the world." I was glad Amy and I were living under their roof.

Realizing full well what a fool I was making of myself, I called all over the country to tell my folks, my brother and sister not to come to the wedding. Joanne and Sandra did all the rest. They returned the gifts, contacted the church, notified the guests, canceled the flower order. I hung the bridesmaid dress away, pins and all, beside my wedding dress.

May 4 and 5 were hard days. Joanne forced me to go with her to play tennis on Saturday. Though my head ached and my stomach wouldn't stop quivering, I went. I hated every second of it.

Joanne knew that worry, embarrassment, and

doubt were making mush of my insides. So
ball after ball was slammed in my direction.
Though everything I felt said, "Go away,
be alone, die," I returned volley after volley.
It was all I could do to move, but move I did,
hour after hour. The exhaustion I felt when
we finally drove home was a sweet relief from
the torment in my mind. I slept well that
night.

Sunday was May 6. Jake met me at church. I
knew the day was no easier for him.

"We should be married by now," he
lamented later at Joanne's. We'd been sitting
on her couch for too many silent minutes. The
sun sparkling off the ocean in the distance was
out of tune with the discord in the room.

"Oh, Jake, it'll be all right. We can work it
out, really we can," I urged.

"We could have made it if they hadn't
interfered!" he spat out bitterly.

I didn't know what to say. I was grateful for
our friends' "interference." How could I
explain the knot of fear I'd felt until that
prayer meeting? God had answered my prayers.
He'd shown me his will so clearly I could not
misunderstand. Waiting was his will. If only I
could help Jake see it too!

The next week was listless and dull. Jake
rarely called. I waited, I did not know for
what. I had decisions to make. I needed a job,
an apartment. But more than that, I needed
strength to keep on going. Big gulfs of
loneliness opened up before me even as similar

gulfs lay endured behind me. It was hard to fold up all my dreams of a husband and a home and put them back on the shelf. I'd been alone so long . . . all my life it seemed. I had hoped that being a Christian would change all that. Perhaps aloneness was not so far removed from God as I had thought.

After all, I mused, *who is more alone than he?*

Escape came between the covers of books. I began to read through the Sumners' library. One afternoon as I sat curled up on their family room sofa, I was caught and held by the story in a little paperback. *God's Smuggler* by Brother Andrew is a true story of a Dutchman who smuggles Bibles behind the Iron Curtain. Anywhere there is a need for God's Word, this man is willing to go, armed only with his faith in God and the power of the Holy Spirit.

Oh, to have a faith like that! A new kind of hunger burned within me. I gazed out the big glass doors to watch the sun make designs on the patio through the leaves above.

Lord, I want that kind of faith, I voiced my yearning. *Whatever it costs, I don't care, but God, please build that kind of faith in me. I don't want to be wishy-washy about you.*

I sensed as I prayed that I was asking for a depth of life that was awesome as well as frightening. I went on. *I know I don't trust you. I know I should and I'm sorry I don't. I've never been able to trust anyone before and I guess I just don't know how.* Old scenes and faces, smiles and promises drifted back across the years. *But, God, I want to trust you. So please help me to.* It was with great hesitation that I placed my hand in the hand of my adoptive heavenly Father.

The headaches and listlessness stayed with me day after day. Joanne finally convinced me to see a doctor. I'd never returned to Dr. Leeds for my six-week postpartum exam, so I decided to kill two birds with one stone. I hoped he would give me some sedatives.

A few days before my appointment I was driving my blue VW bug into town. As I waited at a stoplight, my thoughts turned idly back to Brother Andrew and my prayer for faith.

Then God spoke. He had not spoken in the old way to me since he'd sent me to the adult Sunday school class.

"Meg, of the two alternatives open to me, which would increase your faith more?"

Time and place dissolved as I strained to understand his question. *Oh, God,* I groaned as I saw the picture—my prayer, my sin with Jake, the headaches and nausea. I saw again the glass window shielding babies in their bassinets and tiny blue eyes looking intently into mine.

Oh, God, isn't there any other way? I gasped.

With indescribable sadness, he said, "What other way is there that isn't going to hurt?"

My eyes focused on my hands, clenched on the wheel before me. Tears were streaming down my face.

OK, God, I whispered, realizing he intended to break me, *if that's what you've got to do, do it!*

Only a moment was left for the finality of my acceptance to register in my mind before the stoplight changed to green. Returned to time and space, I drove slowly through the intersection.

Through
the Valley

I spent the next four days trying to convince myself I'd heard God wrong. In the moments I could not escape the thought, I prayed he'd change his mind.

Two days before my doctor's appointment I met a local pastor downtown and drew him aside.

"What does God say about abortion?" I asked him.

He looked at me and cleared his throat. He knew me slightly, saw the engagement ring on my finger. "Well, the Bible doesn't really talk about it. I, ah, you don't think you . . . are, do you?" He glanced nervously at me.

I looked down at the sidewalk. "I don't know, maybe."

"Your fiancé?" he asked.

I nodded.

"I think we'd better pray," he said quickly

and put a hand on my shoulder. I do not remember what he said.

I walked away deep in thought. "Abortion . . . no one would ever know . . . not Jake, not my folks, not my friends, no one . . . but God and me." I grimaced at the truth. "That's One too many."

I sat in my car and tried to sort through the conflicting pictures in my head. Then I remembered Sarah and understood it all.

Lord, if you can put a baby in Sarah's womb, you can take one out of mine without any help from me. I took myself out of your hands once; that's why I'm here. I'll not do it again.

The day before the appointment, I went to Joanne. She looked grave as I related what I feared.

"Let's make sure before we accept this thing," she advised. She laughed ruefully. "Remind me not to pray for faith, will you?"

Moments later, I grabbed her arm. "You don't think I'm being punished, do you?" I asked as a horrible thought crossed my mind.

"God help us if you are," she replied. "If we all got what punishment we deserved, there'd be few Christians around to tell the Good News."

She turned to me slowly. Joanne was tall with short black hair and piercing brown eyes. She spoke seldom as a rule, but when she did, people listened. I could almost hear the wheels turning in her head. "Meg, you asked the Lord to do an extraordinary thing . . . you asked for a faith that would take you through the gates

of hell and back." Her gaze softened. "You did
give God the means to answer that prayer."
She paused and looked out over the ocean.
"But punishment, no . . . not punishment."

Then she spoke words of prophecy that
girded me for the long journey ahead. "I
believe God intends to bless you through all
this, Meg. There's a verse in Romans that says,
'All things work together for good to those
who love the Lord and who are called
according to his purpose.' Only God could say
'All.' "

Joanne went to the doctor's office with me
the next morning. I paced back and forth
across the waiting room. I could not sit quietly.
Finally my turn came.

Dr. Leeds was a gray-haired, handsome man.
He had become a Christian only a year before.
He'd been my doctor for years and I'd noticed
the softening of his mien, the new gentleness
in his voice. He had gone through the last
pregnancy with me, seen what it had done.
Since he knew I was a Christian now, facing
him seemed almost impossible.

He was busy that morning and looked
hurriedly at my chart as I sat on the edge of
the examining table. "What seems to be the
problem, Meg?"

I tried to talk but couldn't. My attempts to
speak caused him to turn and face me. "I . . . I
don't know," I stammered. "I mean,
something's wrong. I . . . I haven't been feeling
too well lately and I hoped you could give me
some sedatives." I dared to glance up at him.

His visage had tightened. He called a nurse in for the examination. I held her hand tightly as the minutes ticked by.

Dr. Leeds let out a low sigh and turned his back to me. "Meet me in my office," his voice was hard. I grabbed his arm as he strode past toward the door.

"What's wrong, Doctor?" I demanded. The flood of blackness began to rise. He took my hand off his arm and looked away grimly.

"What's wrong?" I screamed, shaking now.

"You are six to nine weeks pregnant," he said and turned to leave again.

The flood rose to drown me. "No!" I screamed. "No!" and I struck out at him. Both Dr. Leeds and the nurse restrained me as I screamed hysterically and fought against the smothering darkness that closed above my head.

Once it was over, I lay gasping for breath, facing the wall. The nurse had begun to pray. Dr. Leeds' hands were on my shoulder.

"It's going to be all right," he said and took a deep breath. "I want to talk to you in my office. Rest a bit, then come." He instructed the nurse to stay with me and help me dress.

I remember sitting before his desk. My eyes traced the grain lines in the wood. Between catches of breath I murmured over and over, "What am I going to do? What am I going to do?"

Dr. Leeds waited. "Meg," he tried to lift my eyes with my name. "Meg," he tried again.

"What are people going to say?" The

realization of what I faced began to widen.
"Oh, Doctor, what will they say?" I saw
everything: respect, friends, love, hope, the
new life Christ had given me—all gone.

Dr. Leeds' words caught me then and held
me. " 'Let him who is without sin cast the first
stone.' No one is going to say a word."

"What am I going to do?" I asked him then.
He looked at my chart.

"The boy—you gave him up, didn't you?"
he asked.

I nodded dumbly. "He's up north, in a
Christian home."

"Meg, you've got decisions to make and you
can't make them all now. You were going to be
married, weren't you?"

"Yes," I answered, "but I haven't seen him
lately. We called it off, you know."

Dr. Leeds came around the desk and took
my hands. "Trust God, Meg," he urged me as
he led me to the door. "Trust him. You won't
ever regret it." I leaned, sobbing, against his
shoulder and he held me there, as a brother, a
father, as Jesus would have, until I could walk
down the hall.

Joanne's eyes met me as I came through the
door. One look told her everything. Her
shoulders bowed beneath the weight of the
knowledge. She held my hand as we walked
silently to the car.

"You'd better drive," I whispered.

She drove swiftly down the streets, thinking
hard. I gazed out the window as though I'd
just arrived from a different planet. The world

looked different, far away. I kept thinking how wonderful it would be to die . . . not the horrid thoughts of suicide that I'd fought back on Victoria Street; no, these thoughts came as a promise of sweet release. I laughed as only the dying can laugh. I didn't care anymore . . . living, dying, what did it matter?

My low laugh jarred Joanne from her thoughts. She knew I was far, far away. Mercilessly, she yanked me back.

"I know it's hard, but you're going to have to put it aside for awhile, for a few hours, at least. We're having eleven people to dinner tonight, and frankly, I need your help."

Supper? Oh, yes, supper. I resented having to think of such things. I didn't understand why.

Once home, she grimly forced job after job upon me. The table had to be set, flowers cut, a salad made, detail after detail, until the hours passed. I found myself at the dinner table and was shocked to see a white face looking back at me from the mirror on the opposite wall. I do not remember eating.

Joanne called the Schobergs. The others came too, the Rogerses and the Myerses. I faced them in my shame. They knew about the sin but had never dreamed this would come of it.

"What do you think I should do?" I asked them, unable to look at them. "I want to go away . . . Texas . . . somewhere . . . a home for unwed mothers. I don't want to stay here, to face those people at church!"

Bill Schoberg answered for them. "You can't

go through this alone, Meg. We're your family. God gave you to us. Stay here, we'll help you get through it."

John Sumners, usually reticent, brought up the thought that hung over us all. "What about Jake?"

"He'll have to be told," I said simply. "But I don't see how this changes anything. Marriage to him is no more right now than it was before."

They seemed relieved. John and Joanne offered their home to Amy and me for as long as we needed it. The group agreed then that my financial needs should be met through welfare.

"At least we'll get some good out of all that tax money," Darrell concluded as they rose to leave.

Joanne asked me to help her clean up. When I finally walked back to my bedroom I was exhausted. I fell across the bed. The thoughts would come now. I knew they could not be held off any longer. Numbly I turned on the little lamp beside my bed and tried to brace myself for the battle ahead. My gaze fell on a little envelope propped up against the lamp. Two twenty-dollar bills fell out onto my lap along with a note.

Trust in the Lord, and do good;
so shalt thou dwell in the land,
and verily thou shalt be fed.
Delight thyself also in the Lord;
and he shall give thee the desires

of thine heart.
Commit thy way unto the Lord;
trust also in him;
and he shall bring it to pass.

Psalm 37:3–5

I fell on my knees beside the bed and wept until there were no more tears.

Thus the journey began. I went to see Jake, but his apartment was empty. He was gone. A letter I sent to his parents' address was never answered. I finally took off the engagement ring and put it in the little black box beside the shiny wedding band.

I kept attending Friday Night Fellowship. By the evening I first wore a maternity dress, the news was out. No one said a word. I was treated as before. Only once after a meeting as I walked to Sumners' car did a high school girl confront me.

"How could you do such a thing?" she asked, hurt.

I had no answer. "I . . . I guess I'm just no good . . . a sinner," I told her. "I don't have any excuse. But I believe the Lord will use this in my life. It'll be all right." I spoke more to myself than to her.

"But pregnant! How could you be such a fool!"

I whirled to face her, angry now. "What are you saying?" I shouted. "That getting pregnant is my sin?" I couldn't believe what I saw in her face. "Fornication is the sin . . . but nobody would have cared much about that if I hadn't gotten caught!" I turned away, then said slowly, "Well, God cared, and that's been dealt with, that's over. This

. . . this is something I'm going to have to live through, that's all."

Joanne and John came then. Totally spent, I climbed into the car.

"You're going to have to forgive them, Meg," Joanne said later at my bedroom door. "Don't be bitter. There will be some who won't understand. Let God deal with them." She closed the door softly as she left and I was alone again, facing the darkness in my mind.

Even sleep was no escape, for then the dreams would come. One night I dreamed I was in an endless corridor that had babies' bassinets lining each side. I was running from baby to baby searching their faces, looking for my son. They all looked the same. They all looked like him. "Which one is my baby?" I called out. The faceless nurses did not hear or heed me. Then Chris, the baby's father, was beside me.

"Where is my son?" he demanded. "What have you done with my son?"

"I'll find him, I'll find him!" I cried and rushed back to my searching. I woke from that dream wet with sweat and shaking with cold. I walked out into the quiet, dark living room.

The night was clear, the stars were bright, the moonlight reflected off the ocean. In the stillness of the hour I could hear the surf singing its song.

O Lord! I whispered, reaching out to him, *I love you.* I sensed his presence in the room as I stood there looking out over the ocean, my hand resting on my bulging stomach. The baby stirred within me and the old ache came back . . . the ache to hold my son.

O God, help me, I breathed as I laid my head against the cold glass window.

I went back to my room and picked up my Bible to continue reading where I'd left off earlier, in Isaiah 54. The Holy Spirit wrapped the words of the verses around my heart.

Fear not; for thou shalt not be ashamed:
neither be thou confounded;
for thou shalt not be put to shame:
for thou shalt forget the shame of thy youth,
and shalt not remember the reproach
of thy widowhood any more.
For thy Maker is thine husband;
the Lord of hosts is his name;
and thy Redeemer the Holy One of Israel;
The God of the whole earth shall he be called.
For the Lord hath called thee as a woman
forsaken and grieved in spirit,
and a wife of youth, when thou wast refused,
saith thy God.
For a small moment have I forsaken thee;
but with great mercies will I gather thee.
In a little wrath I hid my face from thee
for a moment, but with everlasting kindness
will I have mercy on thee,
saith the Lord thy Redeemer.

For me? I asked the stillness. *You had that written also for me?*

God gave me another gift in those dark days. I had heard of the gift of tongues, a charismatic phenomenon. What I was given did not seem to fit that pattern. On a night when the sadness threatened to explode inside me if it did not find release, I found myself groaning with words I did not know. It cleared the darkness from my mind and released the pent-up anguish in my heart. Hour after hour I prayed and groaned, and from that night on, the pain never overwhelmed me again.

Then came the night my ex-husband, Randy, called. I had not talked with him in years. He said terrible things, especially when I shared with him about Jesus. When the line was dead, I sat convulsed with fear. Randy was quite capable of making good his threats. Alone with Amy in the big, empty house, I wondered if I would ever feel safe again.

Finally the Sumners came home. I told them about the call. John was calm when he replied, "The Lord has promised, 'I'll never, ever leave you nor forsake you.' Seems to me one of these days you're going to have to start believing him."

His words hit home. God had not given me the spirit of fear, but of power, and love, and a sound mind. But I had to choose to believe it. I began to understand my will—that capacity in which Christ's victory would either be won or lost in me.

I forced myself into a routine of discipline. I could not allow myself to give in to the freezing restriction in my chest, the urge to sit and look out the window all day, the urge to neglect Amy, to hide from people, the longing to die. Each day I chose a job to do. I'd scrub the linoleum, do the ironing, clean the oven, vacuum the house, paint a room. Some days every ounce of strength I had was used up walking from my bedroom out to the kitchen.

I ached in my loneliness. Surrounded as I was by married couples, some of whom were also expecting babies soon, I longed for someone to put his arms around me, warm me, make me his own. A thought came to me one day that three years would pass before I'd know such warmth again.

Three years! I gasped. *I can't wait that long!*

"Can you wait one year?"

Oh, God, no.

"Can you wait a month?"

Lord, I'm not sure I can even live through today!

"Can you stand the loneliness for one hour?"

I shook my head.

"Ten minutes?"

No!

"Five?"

Five . . . five minutes? Yes, Lord, I whispered, *I can stand it for five minutes.*

"Good," he seemed to say. "Then we'll live through the years five minutes at a time."

In July I was asked to take charge of a weekly luncheon for the church's summer program. I'd go to the church at 8 A.M. every Thursday to begin the food preparation. The luncheons were a success. I was glad the Lord was using some of my restaurant experience. Before the summer ended I was asked to take charge of the food preparation for the community men's prayer breakfast. I told the committee chairman

I could only commit myself through the middle of December. My due date was December 26, a year and a day from my son's due date. I dared not think what lay ahead.

I had no intention of giving up this baby. In fact, I had started collecting little items, clothes, blankets for him to use. I had no doubts that the baby would be a boy.

Darrell sat down beside me at a church picnic one summer afternoon. "Meg, have you considered adoption for this baby?" he asked.

"Absolutely not," I retorted. "What do you think I'm made of?"

"But what about Amy? How are you going to support another baby? Do you want to bring them up on welfare . . . with no father?"

"No!" I threw back at all he said. "You don't know what you're asking. How dare you, a man, suggest so casually that I give up my own child?" Others glanced our way as my voice rose. "It almost killed me last time. You don't know what you're talking about."

Darrell shook his head. "I was thinking of the baby, and of Amy and you. I still think it would be best."

"Darrell, don't you *ever* talk to me of this again. I won't give up this baby! I won't. I can't go through it again."

"If God asked you to give him up, would you then?" he asked quietly.

I looked at him closely. How would God ever do such a thing? He hadn't clearly directed me for months. "Yes," I answered, "yes, but only if God asks me to."

By October I knew I had another bridge to cross. My mother expected Amy and me to come home for Thanksgiving. She was so happy I'd become a Christian, an answer to nine years of prayer. She did not know I was pregnant, again. I didn't know how to tell her. I went to Bill Schoberg.

"Have you ever asked your parents to forgive you for all the pain you've caused them?" he asked.

"All the pain *I've* caused *them?*" I asked indignantly. "What about all the pain they caused me? All the times I needed them and they weren't there? All the things I was accused of before I even knew the meaning of their words? What about all that?" I dared him to answer, shaking with anger.

"I'm not dismissing that," he said. "But I'm talking about something else. You have hurt them badly, you know."

I knew. But I sure didn't want to be the first one to say I was sorry.

They started it, I thought, like a four-year-old. *I didn't ask to be born!*

November came. Mom's letters kept asking for an answer. One day as I was walking to the car across the supermarket parking lot, the Lord spoke. I was happy to hear his voice until I realized what he had to say.

"I can tell you what I want you to do with this baby, Meg, and I can tell you through your parents."

I swayed in my tracks. Finally I said, *All right, Lord, I'll write the letters.*

Bouquets
of Love

I wrote the letter to my mother over and over again. Finally I sent it off, all twelve pages. I tried to tell her how I came to be saved, how I met Jake and what had happened. She had planned to come to the wedding, but when it was postponed she'd heard no more about it and had not asked. I asked Mom to forgive me, not only for this new mistake, but for all my rebelliousness through the years. I told her I could not come home.

Joanne brought me a letter a week later.

"You'd better open it," I said. "I'm afraid to read it."

She read it quickly. "They're coming up this weekend," she said. "Here."

I took the letter from her. Mom and her husband would meet me at the San Justin Inn at 1 P.M. on Saturday; that was the very next day.

"I think I'll go shoot myself," I said.

"I'll stick around tomorrow," Joanne said quietly. "It can't last forever."

I prayed desperately all the way to the motel the next afternoon. Amy was so excited to see Grandma that she didn't notice my pallor.

My sister had come also. After rather strained greetings she took Amy for a walk. I sat on the edge of one of the double beds. Mom and her husband faced me.

"A Christian!" she spat out at me. "Why you're no more a Christian than the devil himself."

One dagger thrown . . . a solid hit.

"Oh, Mom, it isn't true!" I tried to defend myself. Anything else, but, oh, not that! They just couldn't tear that from me. It was all I had left. "I do love the Lord, really I do!" I cried.

"You have a funny way of showing it," she replied and turned to look out the window.

Another hit.

I got up to go to the bathroom. My pregnancy, near its eighth month, offered a good reason to excuse myself frequently. Once the door was shut I buried my head in a towel and cried out the hurt from her words until I could stand it again. I splashed water in my face and went out for another round. Her husband started then.

"Are you sick?" he asked. "Can't you stay out of bed with a man?"

Hit, hit, and twist.

"Do you need psychiatric help?"

I sat there shaking my head. "No, no, no. You're wrong," was all I could say. How could I expect them to believe me after all I'd done? All my years of lying to Mom had finally caught up with me. *Two years,* I thought, *two years and then they'll believe me. They'll know I was a Christian, a real Christian today.*

On and on they went. When I couldn't take any more, I'd retreat again to the bathroom and cry into a towel.

"Don't strike back," the Lord kept saying. "Take it, take every accusation. If you throw even one dagger back, the hatred will live on and on. Let it be buried in you. I'll help you. I took it, too."

After about an hour and a half, Mom rode with me back to Sumners'. I wanted her to see where I lived. Joanne was gracious. When Mom began to thank her for taking Amy and me into her home, Joanne replied, "Why not? God doesn't give degrees to sin. In his eyes I'm no better."

Mom could hardly accept that. If I'd been her, I don't know if I could have either.

I drove Mom back to her room.

Before she got out of the car, I turned to say the hardest words I'd ever said. "You're right, Mom. I don't deserve to be forgiven, but I need you . . . I need your forgiveness."

She looked drawn and hard. Losing my dad after thirty years of marriage and then the nine years I'd gone from bad to worse had all left their mark. I loved her then and I knew I didn't deserve her at all.

"Mom, tell me what to do with this baby," I begged. "What should I do?"

"You've never taken my advice in your life!" she rebuked. "How can I believe you'll accept it now?" She got out of the car.

"I will now, Mom. Honest, I will!"

"No," she shouted back. "You never have! You never will!" She turned away and walked to her room.

Joanne put me to bed when I got home. I stayed there for three days.

Thanksgiving that year was also Amy's and my birthday. She'd been born on my twenty-first birthday four years before. Mom sent a card and gift to Amy. Not a word came to me. The Wednesday before the holiday I was sitting on the family room sofa, alone in the house. I heard someone coming up the walk. A florist . . . the same florist who'd been going to do Jake's and my wedding. He had a bouquet of long-stemmed red roses. He stared at my tear-stained face and my enormous figure, jarred at remembering me from months before.

"Miss Meg Tarken?" he asked.

"Yes," I admitted . . . admitted it all.

"These are for you." He handed the flowers to me.

"For me?" I whispered as he left.

I tore open the card. It read:

I love you,
Mom

Joanne found the flowers on the dining room table and hurried to my room.

"She's forgiven me!" I cried. "Oh, Joanne, look!" and I showed her the note. Both of us were wiping away happy, flowing tears.

The next morning, early, I called home. I wanted to say "thank you" for the flowers and all they said.

"It's been awful here," Mom told me. "My life hasn't been worth living since I came home. Everything is going wrong. Things are breaking. My marriage is falling apart. The store is going into a slump. Why, Meg, I knew I had to forgive you . . . for my own sake."

"Do you, Mom . . . have you?"

"Yes, Meg. I love you. This hurts, but we're going to get through it. We'll help you any way we can."

So ended ten years of animosity. The healing had begun. I understood then why Christ told me not to fight back that day. He had wanted the freedom to work.

I asked Mom again what I should do about the baby. She took a deep breath. "I think you should give it up. Amy's been through enough. Don't make life any harder for her. I still can't believe you'll do it, but at least you know how I feel."

I wrote to Dad the next day . . . a short letter. I told him I wished I'd taken his advice when I'd been a teenager. I shared how I'd blown it, and asked for forgiveness, for advice.

A letter from Wisconsin soon came in the

mail. I handed it to Joanne to read. She smiled as she read the first few lines and handed it back.

"It's OK," she said and left me sitting on my bed.

Dad's letter was only one page, but it broke the angry silence between us. It was written in his sprawling, farmer's hand. Yes, he loved me . . . always had. Yes, he forgave me . . . and though he didn't know how or where I'd find the strength to do it, he told me I'd be doing best by the baby if I gave him up.

So it was decided. I had to go through hell again. But obey I would, even if it killed me. I told John and Joanne my decision after dinner.

"Why do I have to go through this?" I wondered later on as we sat before the fire.

John lowered his newspaper and watched me as I rocked back and forth in their big black rocking chair. "Maybe you're the only one around here strong enough. Maybe it's for our sakes. Did you ever think of that?" he asked.

"No," I responded and added, "I wish I wasn't so strong."

I let the word out that I was planning to give up the baby. Through friends I received two anonymous letters, both from Christian couples who for different reasons could not have children. I replied only that I would pray and let them know. I also made contact with a Christian adoption agency in Santa Marta. The woman who interviewed me was cold and crabby . . . sick to death, no doubt, of pregnant girls. I was not impressed, but promised her too that I would pray for the guidance I needed. I could not bring myself to go to the state adoption agency. The last person I wanted to meet was Mr. McJames.

Weeks went by and I still did not know God's will about the adoptive parents. I prayed and prayed. *What if God doesn't tell me?* I thought.

Well, I'll just go to the hospital without an answer, I said to my doubting self. *I don't care if I'm on the delivery table, I'll wait for him to answer.*

Three days later, as I sat reading, I received a tremendous sense of peace about one of the couples who had written me. I knew I had the guidance I'd sought. I do not understand how I knew. But I knew. The next day I called the lawyer who represented them.

"Tell your clients Jesus has a Christmas present for them," I told him. I was to call him when labor began.

The enormity of what I was again facing overwhelmed me at times. I tried to fight through those terrible hours alone. Some nights, however, I knocked on John and Joanne's bedroom door and asked them to pray with me. The days kept going by.

In the middle of December the woman whose advice I'd taken about premarital sex came to see me. She was uneasy.

"Meg," she began, looking away from my bulging figure, "we, ah, I . . . we were wrong. I'm awful sorry!" She clenched her teeth and shook her head.

I took one of her hands. "It's not your fault! I took your advice because I wanted to. You're not to blame. But I'm glad you've changed your mind." I smiled at her.

She nodded and smiled back. "We understand now," she said.

"Good!" I exclaimed. "You know, Romans 8:28 applies to you, too. He said 'All things'; that means even our mistakes. When we give them to God, he can fix them. He can fix anything. He really is God!" We laughed together then and she too was healed.

Christmas came again. This year we had a tree, lights, and laughter. I'd saved every cent I could from my welfare checks to buy Christmas gifts for Amy and the Sumners. I was often tempted to lie to the welfare worker. It would have been so easy not to tell her about the money that had come in the mail or Sumners' offer to lower the amount I paid them for room and board. But each time I resolved to be absolutely honest.

God can't honor a lie, I thought. *He can't bless me if I persist in cheating.* We made it; every month our bills were paid, every need was met. I learned to live without frills.

Christmas morning we were up early. Indeed, John, Joanne, and I were up at 4 A.M., chasing a runaway hamster that was to be one of the gifts. We laughed so hard as we ran after the pesky creature that we nearly roused the sleeping children before we caught it.

Joanne began stuffing the turkey as I made cinnamon rolls for our breakfast. Later, sitting around the beautiful tree opening gifts, I wondered at the contrast between this year and last . . . so much the same, yet so very different.

Gift after gift was passed to Amy. I looked at Joanne with a question in my eyes.

"Don't look at *me!*" she responded. "We've been finding unmarked packages at the door for days now." She reached for a large gift buried under the tree and handed it to me. "I think you've got more friends at the church than you realize."

The package was too large for my nonexistent lap. My fingers trembled as I slipped off the ribbon and paper. Within the tissue was a soft, light blue peignoir set. I held it up with an embarrassed laugh. "Why would anyone give me this?" I asked.

John looked up. "You'll need it someday. I don't think you're always going to be alone."

"It's for your honeymoon," Joanne added. "The day will come."

I didn't hear the conversation for the next few minutes as my mind grappled with the implications of what they'd said.

This isn't going to last forever, I thought, amazed. *It's going to end.*

My due date passed. As December 30 approached I prayed the baby would wait. I did not want my sorrows stacked on top of each other. I went to Midnight Communion Service on New Year's Eve hoping Dr. Leeds would not be there.

January 2, as the household lay sleeping, I

tiptoed to John and Joanne's bedroom door and tapped softly.

"The baby's coming," I whispered. Joanne opened the door.

"I'll dress," she answered quickly, instantly alert. "Get dressed, call the doctor."

I also called the lawyer. He was excited to be able to alert his clients. They had spent Christmas week in San Justin in a motel, waiting.

Later I sat in the lobby of the hospital, a different hospital, one further up the coast, as Joanne went through the admitting procedures for me. A young couple sitting in the lobby gave me a knowing smile.

I shook my head and put my hand to my throat. "Tonsils," I said with a grin and rose to go back to the OB ward.

The nurse got me settled in a labor room. Joanne was allowed to come in.

"The nurse says it'll be a while. I think I'll go home and get some more sleep. Call me when things get going." She smiled and laid a cool hand on my wet forehead.

"I'm afraid," I whispered as I finally faced the reality of what was ahead. "I don't want to go through this."

She brushed away my tears and straightened the locks of hair beside my head. "It's not going to be the same this time. You have the Lord now. It will be different." She squeezed my hand and headed for the door. Before she left she switched off the lights. "Get some rest, if you can," she said and gave a little wave.

I couldn't sleep. The contractions weren't hard yet, but they were not to be ignored. *Lord, I can't do this!* I sobbed there in the dark.

Jesus was near me. "You don't need to, Meg. I'm going to go through it for you. You wait over here until it's over." A deep peace came over me and I dozed.

My dream was more real than the dark labor room. Jesus was holding my hand as we walked through a sunlit glade. He talked lowly, intimately to me there. I don't remember the labor, though I know I went through it. Joanne told me it lasted seven and a half hours. In the delivery room Dr. Leeds laid a baby boy across my draped stomach.

"He's a fine boy, Meg. You did a good job," he said from behind his green surgical mask.

The little black-haired boy screamed lustily. All the months of sorrow and shame faded as I thrilled once more to the miracle of life.

Again I was placed in a room by myself. Later that morning I called for the nurse.

"I'd like to see my son now," I said quietly.

She looked at me in surprise. "Are you sure you know what you're doing?" she asked.

I smiled ruefully. If she only knew! "Yes," I said, "I know." After she left I turned to gaze at the storm brewing outside my window. The wind made fierce threats as the rain was hurled against the glass panes. I steeled myself for the storm and clenched my teeth as the nurse placed the tiny bundle in my arms.

This is it, Lord, I whispered as I pulled aside the blankets. I looked at my tiny son and waited for the searing, the tearing, the agony to begin.

What have you done? I asked the Lord as the minutes ticked away and nothing touched my peace. Then I knew. *You put the maternal instinct in me . . . and now you've severed it!* I was dumbfounded. I was holding someone else's baby. Yes, he was beautiful, but he was not mine. Tears streamed down my face.

Out of the storm God spoke again. "You don't need to cry anymore, Meg. I have all the angels in heaven crying for you."

I held my baby, loved him there as the rain continued to fall outside. But my love did not destroy me; it was a different kind of love than I'd ever known. Finally I called the nurse.

"Goodbye, son," I said as I lingered in my farewell. "You are in God's hands now."

After they left I turned to God again and said, *You spoke to me a year ago in a place like this. Do you have any words for me now?*

I thought then of Mary standing before the angel Gabriel, accepting the most awesome of responsibilities, the most blessed of sorrows God ever asked of a woman. She had answered then, "I am a handmaiden of the Lord. Do unto me as you will."

"*. . . do unto me as you will.*" Her words had become my own.

The next day the adopting parents were scheduled to come for their baby. I had signed all the necessary papers for them to do so. I dreaded the day. *God, will it come now—the storm?*

At noon a nurse came in and I spoke with

her. "Will you tell me when they're gone?" I asked. "I don't want to know when they're here. I'll stay in my room. But tell me when they're gone." I settled down to await the onslaught.

A huge bouquet of flowers arrived. Flowers? For me? Last year there'd been no flowers by my bed. Another bouquet arrived, and another. The phone rang . . . a woman from the fellowship sending her love. Then Marsha Rogers showed up. She'd had no intention of coming, the rain was so fierce, but she couldn't keep from it. We laughed and shared and ate the cookies she'd brought.

I noticed the nurse come in, nod to me and leave. I was puzzled by her action before it dawned on me . . . they were gone! It was over.

The lawyer came to see me later. I don't remember a thing he said, but his face glowed. I knew it was just a reflection of the joy that couple had when the nurse handed them their son. I was happy for them; very, very happy.

Joanne came the next day, a Sunday, to take me home. The heavy rains had left the air fresh, sparkling clean. I walked stiffly to the car through a resplendent world. The sunlight danced through the trees. The birds were making up for all the rainy days of silence, and in a distance, bells from a church were calling people to worship.

"It's like a brand new start," I said to Joanne as we stood looking out over the hills.

"That's what it is, Meg. Time to begin again."

Through
the Valley

February came again. I was one year old in the Lord. We had come a long way together. But now, where?

Do I stay here, Lord? I prayed early one morning. *What is my next move?*

To get a job and eventually move into my own place seemed the logical goal. But I wanted to be certain of God's will. I prayed and fasted. The day I broke the fast I was offered a job working at a local bank.

I'd gone for my interview a study in nerves. I knew I had no experience in banking and my work record left much to be desired. The head of personnel happened to be a Christian. We spent very little time going over my application. The hour was filled with fellowship.

"I hope the pay will be enough for you and your daughter to live on," the woman concluded as she walked me to the door of her office.

Only after I was alone in the elevator did I fully realize I'd been hired. The little cubicle filled with God's presence.

How do I thank you for all you've done? What do I give you?

"Your life, Meg," was his gentle reply. "It's all I want. It's all you have to give."

Amy was provided for, also. A woman from the fellowship who had small daughters offered to care for her. Amy still missed her mommy, but the sting was gone.

I enjoyed my new job, especially the sense of identity that went with it. I was trustworthy now, respectable . . . it was a big change from the aura of suspicion and disrepute that went with cocktail waitressing. The Sumners urged me to stay with them until I was financially secure. We had learned not only to live together, but to love one another. I knew I would be part of their family as long as I lived.

A happy day came, one I'd dreamed about, when I wrote the welfare department, taking Amy and me off the dole. I breathed a big sigh of relief that it was over.

Getting my own place was another stepping stone. I wondered if I was ready, if I could handle the loneliness.

June brought the test . . . maybe this time I would pass.

Tony was a customer at the bank, a successful self-employed contractor. I found his good looks disturbing and I was foolish enough to enjoy the times he'd come to my teller station. I was always left shaken by his steel blue eyes.

One evening after closing, as we balanced our cash, my supervisor noticed Tony's car parked out in the nearly empty lot.

"Wonder who he's waiting for," she asked, smiling knowingly at me. All of a sudden I couldn't count twenties to save my life. Then I dropped a tray of rolled coins onto the floor and hit my knee on an open drawer. By this time the other girls were laughing wildly. I was nearly in tears.

"Here, I'll balance for you," my supervisor offered and proceeded to count my cash while I sat there trying to figure out what I should do. How I wished I'd washed my hair the night before!

"There!" my supervisor said as she finished. "Here, sign out and go lock up your stuff." She followed me into the vault and caught a glimpse of my face. "You look fine," she assured me. "Go and have a good time. Tony is a neat guy. I wouldn't mind going out with him myself."

I couldn't voice my real fears. What if he's not a Christian? Then what?

Tony flicked his cigarette away as I approached. I was glad I'd parked my car out front that morning.

"Hi," he smiled lazily at me. I wondered if he knew what havoc those eyes wrought in me. "I was hoping to take you to dinner tonight."

Oh, why hadn't I washed my hair?

"That would be fine," I answered. "Do you mind following me home so I can change?"

The drive to Sumners' was empty of thought. Joanne was busy in the kitchen when we came up the walk. I made the introductions, then hurried back to my room. Amy watched me put on a pretty dress, then darted out to peek at the stranger who was taking Mommy to dinner.

I wasn't sure of Joanne's thoughts as she waved us goodbye and wished us a pleasant evening.

We didn't go far that night, just to a little Italian place in town. I was uneasy being with him. I had not been on a date in over a year. I wondered how to bring up the subject of faith and finally resorted to my characteristic bluntness.

"Do you believe in Jesus Christ?" I asked him.

We were sipping our wine, waiting for the entree to be served. Tony looked directly at me. "Yes," he said, "I do . . . in my own way."

"In your own way?" I asked. "How's that?"

"I've lived on the sea for years," he replied. "I've made my living there, matched my strength against her." He chuckled. "I've almost lost a few times, too."

He looked away then—out the window—out to the sea he loved so well. "I know there's a God. How could I help knowing, being out there night after night? Men think a lot when they're out on the water." He looked back at me and smiled.

"But do you go to church?" I asked and wondered if I was asking the right question.

"Yes," he said, "but my church does not have walls." The waiter came then. We did not talk that way again all evening.

Tony came for me several times a week after that. Our dates were so different. Often we took Amy with us. He took me back up to the hills and told me what San Justin had been like when he'd come there as a boy. One night we sat on a bluff overlooking miles of shoreline. He taught me how the pilots navigate by choosing landmarks. I began to taste the salty air with a new feeling for the lonely beauty of the sea.

"Why did you ever stop . . . why come to shore?" I asked one night. He told me then of his ex-wife. The empty nights, the fearful watches had been too much for her alone with the child. When Tony lost them he'd sold his boat and sworn he'd never go back out again.

He listened when I explained my relationship with the Lord, but he did not seek such a thing for himself. We argued over the Bible, and I'd point out verses to back up my statements about Christianity. *He may know God,* I thought, *but he sure doesn't know God's Word.*

We attended church together occasionally. Folks said we made a handsome couple. I was uneasy looking at my favorite window in the sanctuary. I wanted Tony to know Jesus as his Lord. The Lord was always the issue between us. But I was beginning to love again and I dared to hope.

We attended a Christian music concert one Saturday night. The message in the music spoke deeply to me. Oh, how I yearned to stir the fires in Tony's heart for Jesus! We walked silently to the car. As he opened the door for me, my shoulder brushed against his. His strong hands gripped my arms as he turned me to him and drew me into an embrace. My heart beat like a trip hammer. It had been so long since anyone had held me, since I had been able to draw from someone else's strength. I began to cry as he held me in his arms until he kissed the salty tears away. He had not kissed me before.

I floated through my days. The troubled thoughts kept getting pushed farther and farther away. One afternoon on my lunch hour I went to the local Christian bookstore. The woman behind the counter knew me from church. She was a Bible study leader there.

"Well, hello, Meg," she greeted me. "Say, who's that fine gentleman I saw you with at church Sunday? He's quite a fellow."

I was embarrassed and kept my attention on the rack of books before me. "Oh, that's Tony," I replied. "We're seeing a . . . lot of each other these days."

"Is he saved?" she asked then, and my carefully constructed facade crumbled before her question. She waited for an answer. I had none to give.

"He is saved, isn't he?" she spoke again, coming out from behind the counter, her concern showing in her face. "Why, Meg, you know God's Word. You know he forbids the unequal yoke!"

I fought back, but the wind of truth was blowing and my little card house collapsed.

"He's a Christian in his own way!" I said desperately.

She looked at me with adamant severity. "There's no such thing as missionary dating, Meg."

I turned and fled. The sea . . . the sea . . . I longed to sit again with Tony by the sea. I drove to the pier, the one Amy and I had walked down for years. This time there was no little girl skipping at my side, but a specter on the one hand and the Holy Spirit on the other.

"Compromise," the specter hissed as I walked, as though driven, down the wooden planks. "No one will ever know. You're on your feet now. Why go all the way with God? Don't you know what it will cost you?"

"Why do you call me Lord, Lord, and do not the things I command you?" came the unflinching question.

"Your friends will still love you. You won't lose anything. You don't have to be a fanatic about this Christianity business."

"He who puts his hand to the plow and looks back is not fit for the Kingdom of heaven."

But, God, I screamed far out to the sea, *I love him! I hate being alone. I can't stand it . . . I just can't stand it anymore!*

"It is better for you to have never known the way of salvation than to have known it and turn from it." He would not back down. He would not relent on his demand for all my life.

Leave me alone, God! I hurled back, angrily. *You ask too much. I* will *have him. Just leave me alone.*

God did leave me alone somehow. Something went out of my life. Like a dog returned to his vomit, I began asking for a cocktail when Tony took me to dinner. Soon I was reaching for his cigarettes when we were together. An old hunger for narcotics returned, a strong desire to get stoned and just forget the whole thing.

One night, walking as we often did along the sand, he took my hand and stopped me. "I love you, Meg," he said simply, his steel blue eyes flashing, deep and full of love.

"Oh, Tony, where will this end?" I whispered, as he held me in his arms, shielding me from the cool sea breeze.

"Well, I expect it'll end at an altar," he said. "That's where it usually does." He sealed his proposal with a kiss.

I was happy in Tony's love. But a part of me I'd never known existed was in a vacuum. I was alone in a new way. I hardly dared think about it.

The Sunday night Bible study at church was held in the sanctuary the evening I went back. I hadn't been going much lately. I'd decided to go in spite of Tony's invitation to come to his place to watch TV and play cards. I had a hunger and a fear that drove me to a place of reckoning. I knew the power of God. I had experienced it in my life. Did I really want to make myself God's enemy? Was I so foolish to think I could oppose him and come out ahead?

A college girl began to sing a love song she'd written to the Lord. Her words wrapped around my heart and freed the words I had longed to pray for so long. I could rationalize myself to anyone, but I could not escape the fact that I was far, far away from the One I loved, really loved. The song went on and on, and before the last refrain, the war was over.

O Jesus, I cried back in the darkness of my pew, *I can live without Tony, but I can't live without you. Forgive me for ever thinking I could.* I knew that cutting out the cancer of sin would not be painless. But the tumor was benign and I knew the Surgeon who held the scalpel.

I wrote a note to Tony trying to explain why I couldn't see him anymore, why marriage was impossible for us. I left it in his mailbox. He did not answer the door. I knew I could not allow myself to ever go there again, nor could I call him. *The rest,* I thought, *God will have to do.*

I walked alone out on the bluff near his apartment, one on which we'd sat and dreamed of our home together. I felt as though some giant hand was crushing my heart in an iron fist. I knew what this would do to Tony. I only hoped he'd realize my own heart would not escape.

A week later Tony's account closed at the bank. He'd sold his business. A friend of his told me he'd bought a boat and had gone back to the sea, to the love he knew. Never before had loneliness been such a cross.

When it was over, when I knew Tony was gone, I knew the time had come for me to leave Sumners'. I could be trusted now. I had passed the test.

Three weeks later Amy and I moved out of Sumners' home. I found a brand new apartment near the center of town. A Christian family lived in the three-bedroom apartment above me and a dear elderly lady lived in the twin one-bedroom apartment beside me. I left Amy's old crib in the Sumners' garage. We had no use for it anymore. Joanne and I were close to tears when I drove away with the last load of my belongings. We laughed at ourselves. One would have thought I was leaving town. I had asked them if Amy and I could stay for six days; we'd been there over fifteen months.

That evening, my first night in the apartment, I knelt in the darkened living room and consecrated my home to Jesus. I knew the way ahead led to a desert. Loneliness had driven me all my life. It could drive me no more, for finally I had accepted the freedom only crucifixion to self can give.

To the
Desert

It was fun making that apartment into a home.
I enjoyed hanging my pictures on the walls,
putting my linens neatly on the shelf. Things
I'd had in boxes at Sumners' those fifteen
months were washed and put away. My own
kitchen again!

I'll bet Joanne is glad to finally have hers back, too, I
thought, *though she never seemed to mind.*

I didn't have much furniture, not nearly
enough to fill the empty living room. I bought
plants instead. Some friends from the
fellowship gave me a rocking chair.

*How did they know I've always wanted one? Only
thing I need now is a fireplace,* I thought. A big
bean-bag chair (another gift) completed my
seating arrangement.

Eventually I bought stools for the open bar
area between the kitchen and the living room
and also made a table from a large empty cable

spool that I had had cut in half. I also bought a single-sized water bed for myself.

Enough of this cold bed business, I thought as I set the thermostat. Amy's single bed was across the room from mine. We shared the single closet and clothes dresser. She was delighted with the new arrangement.

Another friend from the fellowship gave us a score of Christian records. Many were the nights that music filled the void of my solitary hours.

I had prayed that the peace of my home would be evident to all who came there. God answered that prayer, for person after person remarked on it.

The hum of the refrigerator was the only sound as night after night I curled up in my bean-bag chair and read the Bible. I looked for the verses that seemed stamped with my name. Though the ache of being alone lay like a dead weight in my chest, my silent nights were filled with the healing, rebuilding love of God. Christ had given me a cross only to lift me to the Father. Why had I fought against it so long? His only purpose was to bless.

I sang a new song.

To hold more joy than I now have
Would need that I invade the sky
That I might dance from end to end
And never touch again old places.

So this is what life is all about, I thought, adding to God: *You are all there is.* I smiled and waited in the silence. *You knew from the beginning I would look for you in other arms.*

I read all I could find about Mary Magdalene. I understood that woman; cheap, loose . . . no; lonely, empty, hungry for a love that would not go away, turn cold, or drop her to break into a thousand, a million pieces.

Oh, Mary, I thought, *we'll talk one day, but thank you for your search. There are so many of us here, hungry like you.*

Mary had sat weeping in the garden after Jesus had been dead awhile . . . alone once more, so she thought, and unable to rise again. His corpse was all he'd left her and so, that unseen sunny morning, she'd begged the gardener to tell her where it had been taken.

"Mary," he'd called. "Mary," and his voice tore across her years, blew away the ache that had made life intolerable.

"Adonai!" she'd sobbed as she clung to him, to the Man who was God—the only Man who loved her, really loved her. Never, never, never let him go! As she touched him, tears changed for Mary, for she understood at last all his words about himself.

"I must go to my Father," he'd said gently. Then her hands could loosen, for she knew . . . touching him was not as important as having him . . . and he would never leave her again. Mary well knew she was not just what she seemed. Neither was he. They were united . . . spirit to Spirit, the reality of Mary to the reality of God. Such unity is called the indwelling of the Holy Spirit, but for Mary and for me it was and always will be a wedding.

"I am married unto you," he had said through Jeremiah.

That means you have to take care of us, Lord, I reminded him. He knew being alone frightened me at times. The things I knew about the occult because of Jake assaulted me with threat after threat of destruction. I guess that's why God sent the angels. They were visible only as three short streaks of light. I would "see" them only at unexpected times, never when I wanted to. I had read in the Bible that Christians have angels helping them, so I believed they were real entities, personalities with names.

Maybe I'm not really seeing them, I mused one night. *Maybe it's like when God speaks to me . . . I don't think anyone else can hear him when I do.* I couldn't figure it out scientifically and I wondered if that was why I was afraid to share the recurring experience.

Why is it so hard to believe? I wondered. *The reality of who Jesus is is a lot tougher to accept, really.*

At any rate, credible or not, my "angels" (those three shafts of light) were visible to me again and again. I began to realize God meant every word he said. I was not alone. My defense did not depend entirely on me. As a young woman alone with her child in the city, I found great comfort in that knowledge.

Amy started kindergarten that first year of my job at the bank. My baby girl was growing up. She asked hard questions in those days, questions like:

"Mommy, do I have a daddy?"

I told her about her father carefully, not wanting her to hate him or be obsessed with him either.

"Why doesn't he live with us like Sarah's daddy does?"

How does a mother explain divorce to a five-year-old? I stumbled through. I tried to explain why he never came to see her, that he had another wife now, another family.

"Do you think Jesus has a daddy for *me?*" she asked, and her question began a little game that brought us through the years.

"Yes, Amy, I think he does."

"I wonder what he looks like," she said.

"Well," I went on, warming to the building of hope in my little one, "maybe he has red hair."

"Oh, no!" Amy shouted, aghast. "Eric has red hair and he always teases me!"

"Well, maybe he has brown hair," I offered as an alternative.

"Yeah," she returned, "like me."

"What do you think he does for a living?" I asked then.

"Maybe he works in a bank like you, Mommy."

"Yes, or maybe he's a policeman like Jessica's daddy."

So on and on we'd go. When winter came, we'd sit in the darkened bedroom and look out at the stars.

"Do you know that your daddy sees the same stars we do, Amy?"

"He does?" She looked at them more closely then, her chin resting on her hands. "Do you think he lives close by but just hasn't found us yet?"

"I don't know, sweetheart. Maybe he lives in snow country."

"Ohhh," she shivered. "Do you think he has a doggie he talks to?"

"Maybe," I said.

"Does he have a fireplace?"

"Maybe . . . and maybe he's sitting in front of it right now wondering about us."

"Oh, Mommy, I hope he finds us pretty soon!"

For her sake, so did I.

The nights turned into days and weeks and months. Night after night she'd crawl into my bed to dream with me about a day I prayed would really come. I knew that hope carried a corresponding ache with it, but I chose to have her experience that rather than leave her without a hope.

The only other thing that broke the glassy stillness of those days was an occasional call from Darrell to accompany him to speak to a girl or girls in trouble. One such opportunity came in the fall of the first year of my job. One Sunday morning I was to give my testimony at a home for unwed mothers run by the Salvation Army far up the coast. Darrell had also arranged for a singing group of college students to be part of the Sunday morning service.

The small chapel filled with expressionless

faces that all said the same thing. The girls were young, some could not have even been fifteen years old. They were all well into their pregnancies. Their chatter seemed to bounce from happy anticipation of their babies to confusion, hurt, and bitterness.

There I stood, so slender and well-dressed by comparison. I wondered if I could ever hope to find the right words to say. I prayed, then began.

"Two years ago I could have been sitting where you are sitting now . . ." and on and on I reached for them. Five girls stayed behind that day. They wanted to know Jesus. On the way home I realized the magnificence of God; he doesn't waste anything.

Christmas 1974. I had a tree and played all my Christmas music over and over again. Mom and her husband came to spend Christmas week with us as I had very little time off from work. It was good to feel the love between Mom and me again. Almost two years had gone by since I'd been saved. Mom now believed I was a Christian. She accepted my conversion as real. She was proud of the changes she was finally seeing in my life. I didn't need to try to convince her Jesus was my Lord; my decisions said it for me. The more I considered the years of my life before I found Christ and that first year afterward—ten hard years—the more I wondered how Mom had ever endured it. As I looked at Amy and trembled with love for her, I could only pray

God would spare me times like that.

When they had gone home, I had other
birthdays to remember. My boys were one and
two years old now. Seeing little fellows
toddling beside their mommies always sent a
cold shaft through my heart. A lady at church
had children the same ages as my boys. I'd
look for them as the months went by, trying to
see in them how my boys might look. I knew
in that week from December 30 to January 3
that somewhere people were celebrating. Those
days never passed easily for me. I could only
cry for them. Missing them often left me
sobbing on the carpet beside my big table. The
Holy Spirit was there, but he had no arms to
comfort me, no shoulder for me to lean on.
The empty, silent living room simply waited
for the sorrow to pass and for morning to
come.

Someday, Jesus, it will go away, I thought. *Someday
I'll see them again . . . when you come for me . . . when
it's all over. You'll meet me with a little boy's hand in
each of yours. They'll thank me then, Lord. They'll say,
"Thank you for going through with it, for giving us
life."* It was true. I knew it, and seeing it afar
off helped me through those empty, empty
nights.

I stopped attending singles' Bible studies that
next spring. I'd gone occasionally, and each
time I'd questioned my motives. Finally I quit
playing games.

I'm not going there to study the Bible, I admitted.
*I'm going to check out the guys. Well, Lord, if there is
anyone out there for me, you'll just have to bring him to*

me, 'cause I'm not looking anymore. I even changed my hairstyle to the severity of a bun. I didn't want my attraction to be just physical anymore. I laughed at myself in the mirror.

Time became a process of tearing off calendar pages. I'd been at the bank over a year; I wondered if I'd be there the rest of my life.

"One day at a time." The formula still worked.

I began attending a family Bible study on Thursday evenings. I wondered sometimes why I went. Amy would stay awake far past her bedtime and I could not stay alert. But I had committed myself to go and I felt I needed the study, so I continued to go month after dreary month.

In September the rains came again to the little coastal town. I've always liked the rain, especially since the times God spoke to me from out of the storms.

One Thursday evening, as I sat bleary-eyed at the Bible study, listening more to the deluge outside than to the lesson, he did it again. As quietly as the sea receiving the rain, God changed my life. The door opened and a stranger walked in out of the storm.

For
Love
of Daniel

I was determined to ignore him. *Not my type,* I immediately dismissed him. But there he sat, and something about him kept demanding my attention.

Really, God! I fumed inwardly (not yawning now). *He's not my type!*

Silence, but the pressure didn't let up.

Well, I went on silently, *I'm not going to like him. Just because he's a Christian doesn't mean I have to like him!* And with that I refused to talk to the Lord any more that night.

I kept on trying to refuse to like this stranger who had walked into my life, but as the weeks went by I realized I was up against a conspiracy.

Who was he? Dan . . . a physics teacher at a nearby junior college. He was my age, wore glasses, had a moustache. He had just moved to San Justin from the Midwest to take this job for one year.

As time went by I tried to analyze my feelings. The problem was that the more I saw of Dan, the more I listened to him talk and watched him interact with people, the more I realized he had every character quality I ever wanted in a husband. The crazy thing was that emotionally I did not "fall in love." I felt no fluttering of the heart or giddiness in the head. Tony had always left me shaking with just a glance, a smile. With Dan I felt more like curling up in a big armchair and talking about the second law of thermodynamics. Somehow I resented that. I wanted to "fall in love," be head over heels.

Some time later I asked Dan to speak to my Sunday school class. I wanted to hear him relate his faith. He asked me out to brunch afterward.

This guy is a rock, I said later to my picture of Jesus on the wall. *But, Lord, he's really not my type. I don't mind being his friend, but that's it.*

October. Dan had a group of us from the Bible study over to his place for dinner. He fixed pork chops Midwest style—one-inch thick, barbequed. It was an evening of good eating and happy times.

A week later I invited him to dinner.

What am I doing? I wondered that night as I stood out on my little balcony waiting for him to come. The door bell broke my thoughts.

Amy ran to answer it. I came inside to see her standing with Dan holding a tiny bouquet of flowers.

"Here are some for you too, Meg," he said as

he drew a large bouquet from behind his back. Amy was so busy laughing and talking that serving dinner became very informal.

Later Dan walked back with me while I put Amy to bed. He stood there in the darkened room with his head bowed while I knelt by Amy's bed to pray with her. I could see her little eyes wide open, staring at him, wondering, hoping. It hurt to see the hope there.

"Tell me more about yourself," Dan urged as we walked back to the living room. "I don't really feel like I know you. How did you come to know Christ?"

"It's a pretty long story," I said, thinking that would end it.

"That's OK . . . I want to know, really I do." His brown eyes did not waver. I searched them for a threat or sign of falsehood.

I drew a deep breath. "OK," I said. "You asked for it."

Our coffee cups were cold and empty when I finished. The room was full of silence. Dan sat looking at his hands.

"I didn't know it had been that hard. I'm sorry," he said. "You know, it's strange." He looked up. "You see, I've been a Christian as long as I can remember. My dad was a Methodist pastor before he died. On the outside, my life has been spotless." He laughed softly. I didn't understand what he was leading up to and my confusion showed.

"Yeah, I mean spotless. I've never known any of those things you've talked about." He took my hand. "But, you know, I'm just as much a sinner as you ever were."

Something beautiful was happening.

"In God's eyes, thinking about sinning is just as bad as committing it. Did you ever hear of a guy named Oswald Chambers? Well, he said it this way, 'If I've never been a blackguard, the reason is a mixture of cowardice and the protection of civilized life.' Before God, Meg, we're the same . . . sinners saved by grace."

He left soon after that with a simple "Goodnight." I walked back out to my little balcony. I could hear the surf still singing its song.

I found myself turning to Dan more and more after that. He was so steady, so confident in his faith. Next to him I felt like something of a spiritual yo-yo. He never seemed to mind my ups and downs.

We showed up at church together. At fellowship meetings, everywhere we went, I saw approval written in the smiles of those who loved me. It troubled me. Why was I so unsure of myself? I liked Dan, that was certain. But was that love? What was love, anyway? Had all those fiery times I'd known really been love? Had they not left me worse than broken, empty, and betrayed? Was I such a fool that I would value my own emotional response higher than the reality of who and what a man really was?

I guess it's time for me to grow up, I thought.

My dad came west for a visit in November. He met Dan.

"When are you going to marry that fellow?" he blurted out one night at dinner. I blushed clear to my toes.

"I don't know," I faltered. "I'm not sure he's . . . he's . . . I'm scared . . ."

"Good night, girl, you don't have anything to be afraid of in that man!" he exclaimed. How could I tell him I was afraid of what was in *me?* Dad had never liked any boyfriend I'd ever had, and here, without my asking, he'd given his stamp of approval. I wondered at it.

At Thanksgiving time Dan went to my mom's place with Amy and me to celebrate the holiday and our birthdays. Mom and I talked as we washed the stack of Thanksgiving dishes. Ten years ago we'd talked over sudsy water. It was good to be there again.

"He fits right in here, Meg," Mom offered and watched me closely. I was deep in thought and slow to answer.

"Do you think it's all right, Mom?" I turned to her, wanting her to put her arms around me as she had when I was little. She must have known. Moms have a way of knowing, for she did just that. "He's a fine young man, and I can see he really cares for Amy, for you."

I nodded and went back to the sink. Her tactful hope added fuel to the fire.

By December Dan was having dinner with us frequently. One weekend he took us on an outing to a zoo in a nearby city. I had lived in the area for years, but I'd never taken Amy. She skipped around, always coming back to take our hands and walk between us. I gave up trying to figure out how to pray.

Christmas 1975. I tried in vain to celebrate that birthday time of year. I had the tree and all the trimmings, but Dan was gone, and I felt cut adrift. He had flown back to the Midwest to spend Christmas with his widowed mother and brothers and sister.

Lord, what are you doing? I asked the night sky late one evening as I stood out on my balcony.

"I'm going to teach you how to love, Meg. Trust me." Those are the last words I've heard him speak. I bowed before them.

On December 28 Dan came home. After work on the 31st, he called. "How about a walk on the beach?" he asked.

I didn't even bother to change my clothes. Amy, barefooted, raced far ahead of us as we strolled across the hard, wet sand.

"Meg, I love you," he said, "and I want you to be my wife." He paused and looked at me. "Will you?"

I was shaking. He saw it and reached to hold me close. I buried myself in his strong, tender arms. "Yes," I sobbed against all my fears, "I will." He took my hand and I felt a cold metal band slip on my finger. The diamond caught the light and refracted it into a thousand rainbows.

Amy came running up, her hands full of little wiggling sand crabs. "What's the matter, Mommy?" she asked, dropping her treasures.

Dan squatted down to meet her, eye to eye. "I've just asked your mommy if she'll be my wife, and I'd like to know if you'd like to be my little girl."

Amy looked up at me, struck dumb after two years of prayer. I smiled and nodded to her.

"Oh, yes," she shouted and threw her arms around his neck. "You mean you're going to be my daddy?" she wondered.

"Yes, Amy, that's just what I mean."

"Oh, boy, Mom! He's the one! He's the one!" She was jumping up and down. "Say, did you ever have a doggie?" she asked.

Laughing, we walked out onto the pier. This time Amy was on one side of me and Dan was on the other.

Surrounded by love, I thought. The sea was calm and the gulls called to one another overhead. I knew the battle was not over, but for those crystal, sparkling moments, peace had come to my world.

Crossing
the Jordan

The next six weeks were hell. That I could see Dan was perfect for me in nearly every way did not keep my heart from screaming rebellion. How could I marry him if I was not "in love" with him? But hadn't I always mistaken the fire in my veins for love? Hadn't I always been wrong?

O God, how can I know? What should I do? I cried night after night as I paced the floor, twisting the ring on my finger. The decision to marry was not an easy one. I knew this time it would be "Till death do us part."

What was wrong? Was it that Dan was not as tall as I would like, or that he wore glasses? What kind of woman was I, anyway?

One afternoon as I searched God's Word for help, I read in Isaiah the only physical description of the Messiah I've ever found in the Bible. "He has no form nor comeliness, and when we shall see him, there is no beauty that we should desire him."

Why would Jesus be like that? I wondered. *Why would he not choose a body for himself as virile and commanding as the pictures I see, the dreams I dream?* I wondered if God was once again trying to get me past the temporary into the eternal.

Would I have even loved him if I'd lived then? I asked myself and bowed my head in shame. Surely Jesus knew what was in man.

Yet, the battle raged on. By the middle of February I was ready to break the engagement. Dan, ever patient, always kind, exhibited a strength through all those weeks that said much. When he sensed I had reached the breaking point, he suggested we seek counsel. Darrell and Sandra welcomed us, feeling the tension.

I bared my heart to them. There was no help for it, unless I was honest. I felt naked and rather ugly when I'd finished talking.

Darrell addressed Dan, "How does all this strike you?"

Dan's face was drawn. The weeks had taken their toll. "I've never stopped believing Meg is God's choice for me. It hurts to see her going through all this. But, in a way, I'm not surprised. We say we believe in spiritual warfare. Doesn't it make sense that Satan is making one last big play to thwart God's purposes for us?"

I hadn't considered that before. I didn't have the sovereignty of God all figured out yet, but

I sure knew the enemy had power to waste and destroy.

Darrell smiled at us as he took Sandra's hand. "Shall I tell them about our courtship?" he asked her.

We were sitting around their dining room table. The children were playing quietly in the living room. I wanted so badly to find help here, resolution. If I didn't, I wondered what would become of us, Dan and me.

Darrell could read the worry on my face. He smiled at me as though he knew the way out.

"Meg, believe it or not, I know exactly what you're going through," he began. "After I'd proposed to Sandra, I was hit by the immensity of what I was doing. I knew she didn't fit my dreams of the woman I'd marry. Her nose was too short and her hair was the wrong color for starters. But, there she was. I cared for her, I knew that; but, boy, was I scared! Finally I went to Bill Schoberg for help. What I'm going to give you is what he gave me." He turned to Dan.

"By the way," Darrell said to him, "Sandra and I have had a terrific six years together. God has really blessed our marriage."

I could see the truth of that. I'd always seen it, ever since I'd met them years before.

"Bill said, 'Love is not something you feel, it's something you do.'" Darrell waited for that to sink in. "Meg, what do you think about Dan? Do you think he'll make a good husband, a good father?"

"Oh, yes," I answered, "I know he will."

Darrell reached for his Bible. "You've seen what's in his heart, the kind of man he is, right?" he said as he turned the pages.

I nodded.

"Then, Meg, cross the Jordan. Here," he said, sliding the open Bible across the table to me, "in the book of Joshua, see what God said to him."

I began reading through the first chapter.

"Don't stand there on the edge, wondering if Canaan really is a land of milk and honey. Sure, there are giants there to be routed, but God promised Joshua he'd be with him, he'd go before him. He's saying the same thing to you."

The kitchen clock ticked the seconds away as I read and reread the first chapter. The message was clear. God was speaking to me out of his Word.

"OK," I said as I took a deep breath, feeling the darkness recede. I looked at Dan. "I'll cross the Jordan, but I'm not going to wait till June to do it. Could we move the date up?"

Dan smiled a curious smile. "Sure," he replied, "when would you like?"

"I don't know . . . we need time for a honeymoon. You have Easter week off. How about Palm Sunday?"

Dan started to laugh. I felt like kicking him. There I was, going through the pit, and he was laughing!

"What's so funny?" I fumed.

Dan grinned at Darrell and Darrell chuckled in return.

"Dan talked with me earlier, Meg," Darrell explained. "He said he'd been praying you'd marry him on Palm Sunday."

I looked quickly back at Dan. How could I resist this thing anymore? Suddenly, I didn't want to. It was settled.

I laughed with them as I realized it had probably been settled in heaven a long time ago.

Resolution had come. Only one last skirmish disrupted the peace that followed.

One night after Dan had joined Amy and me for dinner, he decided to take Amy downtown for an ice cream cone. Earlier in our courtship I'd told him about my "angels" and described them to him. He'd smiled understandingly and made no comment. That evening he and Amy were no sooner out the door than he came rushing back in.

"What's wrong?" I called from the kitchen, startled.

"They're there!" he exclaimed, amazement written across his face.

"Who's there?" I asked, grabbing the dish towel for my wet hands.

"The angels . . . they're there, just like you said . . . I saw them just outside the door!"

I laughed out loud. "So you don't think I'm a little strange anymore?" I asked, chuckling.

"No," he said, leaving again, shaking his head all the way out.

"Thanks, God," I said with another chuckle as I turned back to the dinner dishes. Five minutes later a strange dread settled over me like an icy claw. I tried to shake it off, but the threat grew stronger. I got down on my knees on the kitchen linoleum and claimed the blood of Jesus on my apartment, on Dan and Amy, and on me. Somewhat relieved, I went back to my work.

A knock sounded at the door. I froze. "Jesus," I whispered. "Your blood covers whoever stands there." I had no way of seeing who waited for me out in the night. For all I knew it was Satan himself.

I walked slowly to the door. *OK, Lord,* I breathed as I gripped the door knob, *I receive this person in the name of Jesus.*

It was black outside. A man stood there. Slowly my eyes adjusted to the dark. A thrill ran down my spine, followed by a tightening in my stomach. It was Tony.

"May I come in?" he asked, his eyes flashing.

I nodded and stepped aside. I knew then why God had let Dan see the angels. Fierce warfare was raging, but God had wanted me to know I was protected against the assault.

I walked back to the kitchen, leaving Tony sitting on a stool on the other side of the breakfast bar. I was afraid to meet his eyes.

"I've missed you, Meg," he said, yearning evident in his voice.

"Tony," I faced him then, drawing a deep breath, "I'm engaged to be married."

He looked quickly away. How I hated myself for hurting him, but what was the alternative?

"I wanted to see you," he said, looking back, rising and then walking around the end of the bar. I prayed hard and fast as I watched him coming. He took me in his arms. A powerful desire to release myself to him tore through my veins. But a strength I knew did not come from me held me fast. Gently I pushed him away.

"No, Tony," I whispered, meeting his eyes, no longer captured by them. "No more. It's all over."

I offered him coffee and invited him to stay to meet Dan. His eyes kept searching for mine, as though he'd known all along the power in them. But I was free at last. As his game continued, I became angry that he still sought to claim me.

Fifteen minutes later, he was gone. The house was empty again, except for God and me. Dan and Amy finally returned. I was shaking as I told Dan what had happened. He held me until I was still.

April 11 was only two months away! Not much time to plan a wedding! Our plans for a small, inexpensive ceremony mushroomed as the guest list grew to over three hundred people. We didn't have much money to spend on flowers. I figured we'd fill the church with friends instead.

Dad promised to come to give me away. He'd waited a long time to do that. When I'd married Amy's father, Randy, we'd gone to Las Vegas. I'd stood before the Justice of the Peace wearing old blue jeans and a sweatshirt. Randy hadn't shaved in two days. How different this would be!

I started sewing a long dress for Amy to wear as the flower girl. I found the veil I'd made three years before and used the material for Amy's pinafore. As I packed up my things to move into the two bedroom apartment Dan had found, I hesitated over the wedding dress I'd made to wear with Jake. Finally I decided to put it in the Goodwill clothing receptacle across the street from Amy's school.

Somebody can use it, I thought as I put the box through the slot that night. The next day when I dropped Amy off at school, I was amazed to see that the receptacle had burned down in the night. I soberly wondered if God had ever intended for that dress to be worn.

I was to be out of my apartment by the end of March. The 31st was also my last day of work at the bank. Dan had always figured his wife would work, but in the months of our courtship, he changed his mind.

"I want you home," he said one weekend. "It won't give us much freedom financially, but I really think being home with Amy is a much better investment of your time."

Amy had stood there listening and she understood. She climbed into my lap, put her arms around my neck, and uttered a little sigh.

Walking out of the bank for the last time was much easier than leaving my apartment. When the last load of furniture was gone, I stood a moment in the empty living room. Twilight brought a hundred memories . . .

memories of Jesus communing with me there in the silence. As much as I'd hated being alone, somehow I didn't want it to end. Loneliness had driven me deep into God's arms. I knew I'd never come out.

Will you send the angels, Lord? I asked in a whisper. I knew somehow he wouldn't, at least, not in the same way. They would be there in the new apartment, but I wouldn't need to see them anymore. I didn't really say "goodbye" as I closed and locked the door behind me. I just turned the last page of a chapter in a book.

I drove with Amy back to Sumners'. Joanne had my old room ready.

"How many days this time?" she asked, her eyes twinkling.

"Ten," I answered, "I hope."

Mom called the next day. "I want to buy you a wedding gown," she said over the phone. "Every girl should have the fun of buying one. When can you come down?"

Mom and I had a great time finding the perfect dress. As we sat side by side watching the saleslady bring out gown after gown for our consideration, I leaned over to whisper to Mom, "White? Are you sure you want to buy me a white dress?"

She smiled at me. "I'm not about to call God a liar. If he says all things become new . . . that you are a new creation, who am I to argue?"

Yes, I thought, *it's got to be white . . . or else the whole picture is wrong.*

The dress we chose was soft, simple, and to me, just a little elegant. Mom had brought my sister's veil for me to wear with it.

I found the bridesmaid dress with the pins still in the hem of the sleeve in the back of one of Joanne's closets. Again we sat at her kitchen table to finish what had been interrupted by a prayer meeting three years before. We were both silent as I took out the last pin.

"Boy, it sure took you a long time to finish that thing," she exclaimed as she rose to get us another cup of coffee.

"Yes," I agreed, "but at least I got it done."

April 11 was fast approaching. Joanne and Sandra took care of detail after detail. Dan's and my relatives began arriving from all over the states. Les came from the East Coast. Without words, he smiled at me amid the rush and flurry. Homes were found for everyone to stay in over the weekend. Gifts arrived with every mail delivery. Mrs. Schoberg gave me a huge shower. The girls at the bank followed suit.

Dan's mother opened her arms to embrace me. She was short and gray haired. Her life had been poured into the Lord's work. Her husband's ministry, her family, her home, all had been enriched by the touch of this faithful woman.

We had very little time alone to visit, to get to know each other. Saturday, the 10th, she asked me to drive her downtown.

"I guess I ought to tell you I had trouble accepting you at first," she said, as we stopped for traffic. "My husband and I always had strong feelings about divorce. We never thought one of our sons would marry a divorcée."

She looked out the window as I drove. I didn't know what to say. How I regretted all the mistakes I'd made!

"But the Lord has undertaken for you," she went on. "A dear Christian friend of mine has recently gone through divorce. I was with her through much of it . . . and you know," she paused, "I've finally realized that divorce is not the unforgivable sin."

I nodded and smiled hopefully at her.

"I'm proud to have you in the family, Meg," she said. "You are God's perfect choice for Dan, for all of us."

There was no rain on my wedding day. After the Palm Sunday church services, a lady asked if she could leave all the palm fronds in the sanctuary despite our wedding in the afternoon. I was glad for the added decoration. An hour before the ceremony I returned to the church to begin dressing. Mom was there to help. Soon people were rushing around, getting in each other's way. Amy stood by in her pretty dress and tiny veil, enjoying it all. In a far-off room, Dan was helping Dad into his cummerbund. "Nothin' but a lousy girdle," Dad fumed, loving every minute of it.

At last the music began. Dad came to the

room where all the women stood watching the veil being placed securely on my head. He and Mom stood looking at each other across the years, the hurt, the anger—and they smiled, a smile that mingled love with regret.

Mom left quickly then to walk in on Les' arm. Dad grumbled about the cummerbund, his eyes red with tears. Then my sister left in her silver gown, followed soon by Amy. I was tempted to step out of the room to watch Amy make her way down the aisle, handing her daisies out, one by one, to the friends on either side.

Dad put his arms around me in the quiet room and held the tears back no more. "I love you, girl," he said, pulling the words from deep within him. "God knows, I always did, but I didn't know how to show you all those years. I'm sorry I wasn't a better father to you. Maybe if I had been . . ."

"No," I cried, tears streaming down my face, "No, Daddy, that's over now. Don't you see? All those years, they brought me here . . . and Dad, I wouldn't want to be anywhere else."

The sound of the wedding march broke us from the embrace, an embrace I'd dreamed of on many dark and fearful nights when I'd wanted to be a little girl again, safe at home, in Daddy's arms.

"Here, help me with this thing," I said, trying to get the veil down over my face. We used up the last of a box of hankies, then laughed as we stepped out of the room.

Dad offered me his arm and we began the

journey on dry ground across the Jordan. *I sure spent a long time wandering around in the desert,* I thought as we slowly passed between the smiles and tears of the people who had prayed and laughed and cried with me, year after year.

I paused as we passed by the window. There he was, there at Gethsemane, the Man who sweat great drops of blood as he prepared to offer himself a sacrifice for the folly, the rebellion, the wasted years of all mankind.

Thank you, I cried in a whisper no one heard, no one but him. *Oh, Jesus, thank you so very much.*

Epilogue

Soon after our marriage, I knew I was with
child again. In September we moved from our
apartment into a new home, our very own,
complete with a fireplace and view of the
distant ocean. I put my rocking chair close to
the hearth.

We drove to Sumners' in November and
brought the crib out of their garage. It was the
last of my belongings to leave their home.

In the middle of December, the pregnancy
showed complications. I spent Christmas lying
on the couch, watching Amy, Mom, her
husband, my brother and sister laughing and
playing together. Amy's greatest gift from her
daddy was his name. Her adoption was
finalized December 23. I had my gift too,
growing and kicking within me.

On December 28 Dr. Leeds sent me to the
hospital to induce labor. He dared not let the

pregnancy continue to full term. A half hour after midnight, he held a baby boy in his arms for me to see. "Here's your son, Meg," he said, his voice breaking.

I looked up at Dan and smiled. He bent to kiss me. "Thank you," I whispered.

The next day, December 30, I asked for my son. The nurse brought him to me.

"Hello, little boy," I said, crying away the ache that had never completely gone away, and I held him tight in my no-longer-empty arms.